MW00489236

THE

ART OF

GETTING

SHIT

DONE

This is a work of nonfiction.

Copyright © 2019 by Georgie-Ann Getton-McKoy

All rights reserved. No part of this book may be reproduced or
used in any manner without the written permission of the
copyright owner except for the use of quotations in a book review.
For more information, address: hello@gsdwithgeorgie.com

Second Paperback Edition September 2020

Book design by Georgie-Ann Getton-McKoy

978-1-7336679-0-6 (paperback)

DEDICATION

I'm the type to say yes to a job, then google how to do it.

Dedicated to family, history, and culture for being my motivation to Get Shit Done.

TABLE OF CONTENTS

FOREWORD

What are the ingredients of a perfect life? It's something I used to try so hard to figure out because I didn't think I had one. See, most of us, like me, went through life thinking we needed the "perfect this", or the "perfect that" to achieve our dreams. When in reality, everything that you need is already inside you.

Have you ever seen the movie, "Friday", with Ice Cube? There is one scene in particular that I want to focus on. Ice Cube's character wakes up in the morning to have a bowl of cereal. He walks to the fridge super excited to tear that cereal up, all he needed was some milk. As soon as he opens the fridge, he discovers an empty milk carton. Frustrated by the lack of milk, he storms towards the trash can to throw the cereal away.

But his father, a very frugal man, stops him in his tracks. And he yells at Ice Cube's character saying, "You better put some water on that damn shit."

While that was a very hilarious scene in the movie, it was a teaching moment, for me at least.

See I grew up in a single parent home; just myself, my brother, and my mother. My father wasn't around, because they got divorced at an age when I could barely speak. And because it was just her supporting two boys who wouldn't stop growing, eating, life for us was not a crystal stair.

I recall a ton of times where I myself went looking for the perfect ingredient like Ice Cube's character but walked away frustrated when I didn't get what I came for.

Ingredient #1: Money.

I always wanted to be an entrepreneur. I used to read expired copies of Forbes Magazine while waiting in the doctor's office, imagining myself one day on the cover. But how was a little black boy from Newark, New Jersey ever going to get there without the money? So, thinking I needed a ton of money to start a business, I'd go to banks to get a loan. Denied. Angel investor groups to pitch my idea. Denied. Friends and family? Denied.

Everywhere I went to get money to start a business I got denied. So, one day, I just started going to the library. While in the library, I would spend hours watching interviews and coding tutorials from entrepreneurs on YouTube, looking for clues or some sort of hint on how I could get started and reach the success that they possessed.

One day, in the library, while browsing Craigslist, I discovered a listing for an internship. It was a perfect way to learn directly from other founders on how I could get started. I didn't have a college degree, but I had this website about video games that I built with a few friends of mine, on the side, while going to the library every day.

To my surprise, they gave me the job, without hesitation. I was curious, as I didn't have a college education like they asked for in the listing. Why did they take a chance on me? And when I asked one of the founders why, he said, "Your website gets a quarter million more unique visitors than ours, can you teach us how to do that?"

I was confused. Here was this man, who seemingly had more money and more resources than I had but didn't have the traction that I unknowingly created on the side, with a few friends. That's when I discovered that while I had no control over money, I had complete control over my time. And because I spent my time every day in the library learning, I created a skill that would then bring me the money that I desired.

Ingredient #2: Luck.

When I was 16 years old, I met Monte Lipman, the founder of Universal Records (now Republic Records). His personal driver dropped him off in an all-black S-Class Mercedes Benz

Sedan in front of my high school. I never saw anything like it. It was a Saturday, and he was the only reason I, or any kid, would show up to school on a Saturday. He was there to speak to students at a special career day. Monte Lipman was the guy who ran the music industry. Artists like Nelly, Lil Wayne, Drake, Akon, and more were under his umbrella.

I had dreams of being in the music industry myself (sidebar, I tried to be a rapper in my past life), so my goal was to network and get some tips. He gave a speech, and before he left, I looked him in his eyes and said, *"this won't be the last time we meet"*. I don't remember anything from his speech except for his formula for getting lucky. It's the philosophy he learned while he was young and got him to where he is in life. So, a curious kid like myself paid close attention. Here's what he wrote on the chalkboard:

Preparation + Opportunity = Luck

It was the first time I had seen the word "luck" in a not so magical way. When you think of luck, it's four-leaf clovers, blowing out birthday candles or throwing coins in a pond. Never did I imagine luck as something I can create with my own effort. But it made sense. According to him, if you stayed prepared and an opportunity arose, you would get lucky.

See, I was a hard-headed kid. And while I did pay attention to those words, it took me years to realize it's the truth. Jealousy, envy, and anxiety plagued me for most of my young adult years, and even till this day, I deal with it in very small doses. But one day, I had to ask myself, why am I jealous?

I had this company I started, and every day I used to write a blog post, *hoping* it would bring me tons of traffic to my website. My co-founder and I would throw events, *hoping* that would get people interested in our products, by seeing it in person. We would reach out to people, who were influential, to interview them, *hoping* they would think we were cool and would make introductions for us. In the end, we didn't sell more products, and we became jealous and we envied the success that our peers were receiving.

Then one day, NYU called and asked us to produce a conference for them. Produce a conference? Why the hell would they think we were perfect to do this? Well, the blog posts that we wrote, while it didn't get a lot of traffic, it was a great deal of valuable content. The events that we hosted, while it didn't help us sell our products, we helped people connect and start their own businesses. And while none of the people we interviewed made connections for us, they themselves loved us and were willing to speak at our conference for free. We had everything we needed, but we were so focused on what we didn't have, we didn't realize that we had built an entire movement with our eyes closed.

That conference has gone on to happen four more times in three different cities. Sold out each and every time. You could say, we got lucky. But all those small things we did just prepared us for that one phone call which was the opportunity. Monte Lipman was right. And what's even crazier is, I blogged about this very story and he found it. Years later I was able to tell him to his face, "I told you it wouldn't be the last time we saw each other".

Money and luck are just a few of the ingredients we think we need to make things happen in our life. We don't need them at all. Truthfully, I thank God I didn't have either in those situations. The things that I would die for, didn't live up to expectations. The opportunities I would kill for, couldn't survive a drought. So, if we don't need those things to be successful, what do we lean on?

I'm gonna cap this off with a bit of science. Studies show that 60% of the human body is made up of water. That means more than half of our body has all we need to get lucky, get money, get success, find love, achieve goals, get that job, move out, the list goes on. We just have to realize that our burdens are just blessings behind curtains. The name of this story is "just add water", but we don't have to add water because we already have it.

When I first met Georgie-Ann, I saw a lot of myself in her. She was someone who had very humble beginnings and faced many obstacles on her path to success. Despite everything she had going on, she never let her shortcomings keep her from taking long shots. She worked many jobs, hosted conferences, organized communities, and built a startup, all while raising her son. I was witnessing a real-life superhero. If I wanted to learn how to be productive, there was no better teacher than Georgie-Ann. Don't just read this book and then move on. Take time with it, take notes, meditate on it. In a time of many distractions, those who actually know how to get sh*t done become the jewels of society. Good luck!

- Anthony Frasier
Author of Don't Dumb Down Your Greatness

PREFACE

Today is August 11th, 2020, it's been 554 days since I published the very first version of The Art of Getting Shit Done.

If you were one of the lucky humans who got a first edition copy you will find many grammatical errors, typos, formatting issues, and much more in the book. I mean I did warn the reader during Chapter 1 of the book. But with all the imperfections I got the book DONE!

I was able to add published author to my list of titles. Since publishing the book I have sold over 300 copies, landed multiple speaking opportunities, went on a book tour, got book publishing/marketing clients, did a TEDx Talk, and much more.

Now I want to release the second edition which has been edited to clean up most of the errors from the first book. AND make it easier to record the audiobook version. Which I have been avoiding because I hate how my voice sounds. Afterall don't we all?... Otherwise, I've left the content of the book the same with the exception of this little note I've added as a preface.

It's mind-blowing to see how much the world and my life have changed since when I published the first edition in February 2019.

It's only been 1 year and 6 months but:

- I am no longer living in Georgia.

- I am getting divorced.

- Oh, and there's a global health pandemic happening (See the history books for COVID 19)

Yea so life is a bit UPSIDE down right now (read more and follow along at gsdwithgeorgie.com or on social media @GSDwithgeorgie) but none the less I still have to keep getting shit done.

Reading my own book again during the editing process reminded me to recenter myself and figure out what comes next for me. There will always be external forces and life will come in the way but how do I want to show up each day? How can I provide value each day? How can I get shit done each day?

With all of these life experiences happening all at once it truly emulates the title of my podcast "Doing the Most: The Misadventures of Entrepreneurship." *Hmm, maybe that should be the title of my next book!*

I hope whoever you are and where ever you are the stories, practices, and wisdom that you are about to read in the pages to follow truly empower you to take action.

If you are a dreamer, I want my words to inspire you to rise up and get shit done.

If you are a doer, I want my words to ignite you to thrive and keep getting shit done.

Getting shit done isn't a science with any magical formulas. It's art! Now go create your masterpiece. Remember you may not always have everything you want, but you always have everything you need.

Good luck!

Georgie OUT!

August 2020

CHAPTER 1

LESS DREAMING, MORE DOING

———∾∾———

> *"Tomorrow doesn't exist, only today, and yesterday"*
> *- Georgie-Ann Getton-McKoy*

In 2016, after hosting my largest event to date, I was on a high, full of gratitude, happiness, and excitement. At that moment, I decided I wanted to share my story - my adventures and misadventures about how I've Got Shit Done throughout my life.

No matter what roadblock life presents, I've been able to look at my resources and circumstances and build ladders to get over each roadblock. Along the way, I learned some life-changing lessons, hack, tips, and tools.

It felt like I would be a lousy human if I didn't share what I learned with others. Whether they would use my stories as motivation, try my hacks and tips, or only gain some insight, I knew it was time I shared it with the world.

I started in 2016 then stopped, then restarted in 2017, then stopped again. This year, 2018, I will finish the book, and in 2019 the world will finally get a hold of "The Art of Getting Shit Done" by Georgie-Ann Getton-Mckoy.

It was time to quit dreaming about this book and invest my resources into doing this book.

It was time to get this shit done!

Hey Reader,

This note is going to be quick and to the point. Here I am at 1:21 am on Saturday, July 15th, 2017 FINALLY writing this guide. I started it November 5th, 2016, after I held the very first Get Shit Done summit in NYC. I would write bits in a notebook, other bits in my phone, more bits on post-it notes. Just a shit ton of bits everywhere. No more bits! I've decided it's time to get in front of the computer and Get This Shit Done.

First, who the heck am I? My name is Georgie-Ann Getton-Mckoy. Yes, it's a mouthful, so most people call me Georgie, and I'm okay with that. I am currently 22 years old, Baruch

College graduate, with a B.S in Graphic Communications as of June 2017, mother to Cameron and Bryanna, and wife to Bryan, Founder of Illicit Mind Inc., Entrepreneur, Diversity in Tech Enthusiast, speaker, and last but not least, the Queen of Getting Shit Done.

Second, why should you read this book? If you want to develop a doer mindset, this is the book you read. I've had to step out of my comfort zone, push my limits, become super resourceful, and literally reprogram my mindset to get where I am today. I want to share that information with you so that you can too. You should read this book if you're going to stop wasting time and start Getting Shit Done.

Third, what to expect... Expect the unexpected! That's what you should expect. A bunch of grammatical errors, whatever Grammarly free version doesn't pick up will stay. Expect a bunch of shits, fucks, damns, and more. I mean you decided to read a book called "The Art of Getting Shit Done", so I assume "sentence enhancers" won't offend you. Expect me to be raw and real. I will NOT be sugar coating anything. If you don't like the truth, well wrong book, sis.

Fourth, we've already wasted enough time. Let's get this shit done already!

CHAPTER

THE GET SHIT DONE MANIFESTO

> *"An entrepreneur isn't someone who owns a business, it's someone who makes things happen."*
>
> *- Timothy Ferris*

I believe that the art of getting shit done is composed of 13 sections. Each section is unique, and if applied correctly, can lead to magical life experiences.

13 principles for Getting Shit Done

Hustle

This means many things, but my definition is, going out into the world and working hard.

Do Good Shit

Doing good things and being a good human being is essential. We were all put on this earth with literally billions of other people. If we help each other, life will just naturally be more comfortable, and more efficient. We will have more people in our corner. I can go on all day. Just do good shit!

Work Smart & Hard

Working 80 hours a week doesn't mean anything unless you are doing it smartly. You have to be making efficient decisions that save you time and energy but get a lot done.

Innovate

Create. Create. CREATE. Always be making something.

Create Change

Change happens if you make it happen. We live in a world that isn't perfect, and it would be boring if it were perfect. Create change every day.

Do What You Love

If you aren't happy, then what are you doing?

Think Big, Start Small

Have humongous dreams and aspirations but start small. Baby steps are necessary because without them, you won't learn how to walk, then how to run. We must remember that we all started as an egg and a sperm. Now we are amazing humans.

Stay Humble, Hustle Hard

Know that no matter how far you get, there is more to go. Celebrate those accomplishments and then get back in the game.

Collaborate

Work with people. There are billions of us. If you want to go fast, go alone, but if you really want to go far, then let's go together!

Make Magic

The formula for magic is [Happiness – Fear]. Take chances, create, be magic, MAKE MAGIC.

Choose Yourself

You should put on your oxygen mask before helping those around you. Self-care isn't selfish. If you're good, then those around you will be good.

Be Ambitious

You must be determined. Things won't always go your way, they won't always go well, and they won't always be easy. But if you are ambitious and have a strong desire to achieve success, you WILL be successful!

Love What You Do

Simple.

CHAPTER

RESOURCEFUL AF

"Everyone accepts that limited resources must be managed yet we fail to recognize that will power is one of them."

- Gary Keller

In life, it's not about what you have, but what you do with what you have. Don't quote me on this. I'm not sure if it's a universal fact, but it is a fact for me in my life. I paid nothing for college. I've made thousands while working from home, I've gotten jobs that I had no experience in, and I've sat at tables where others stared and wondered how did she get here. The simple answer? I'm resourceful AF. This is a gift that I personally believe is wired into my DNA but would have gone dormant if I didn't tap into its power. I think all historically marginalized people are born with this gift, specifically blacks, brown people, women, etc. We were born into a world with cards pre-stacked against us before conception. Like seriously? So, God gives us that gift of resourcefulness, and it is the duty of our nurturers (parents, guardians, family, etc.) to help us to leverage this gift and be great with it. And my family and friends sure did help me in activating this gift.

Let's go back to 2002 so you can start to understand what I mean.

The day was coming close, and I was upset, nervous, and excited at the same time. My mom, two brothers, and a few uncles, aunts, and cousins were about to get on a flight to move to the United States. All we were taking were a few suitcases of belongings, hopes, and dreams. I was only seven years old, so moving to another country, leaving my friends, and other members of the family, which included my dad, did not seem fair. I made sure to let my mom know that she was making a bad decision moving to this America place, but I was brushed off, as she recognized the doors and opportunities that would open up for herself and her three children.

When we landed at JFK airport in New York City on March 2nd, 2002, it was cold outside. Well, at least to us it was. Coming from the island of Jamaica, any day below 85 degrees was cold. We instantly requested sweaters or jackets.

We got picked up by my maternal grandmother and her brothers. They had made space for us to stay in my grand uncle's Brooklyn home, while the adults figured out jobs and other housing arrangements.

Our time in Brooklyn was short-lived, but it was pretty eye-opening. I saw snow for the first time in Brooklyn, took the subway, and started to understand the inner workings of the City. A few weeks later, my mother and brothers went to a new house in Brooklyn, and I moved to the Bronx.

I was in elementary school, 1st grade to be exact, which meant I had to go back to school. My mother sent me to live in the Bronx with my cousin and a family friend. I was a stranger to this country, and now I didn't have my mom with me either. This was my first chance to put my resourceful gene into action.

The family friend I stayed with had a bunch of other kids living with her too. Various nieces, cousins, children, or the children of a friend...like me. I didn't speak or interact too much because it was still very new to me. I got settled into my section of the home and started to prepare to enter the New York City public school system.

Kids are always mean, especially to the new girl with a thick Jamaican accent. I was called the beloved African booty scratcher more times than I could remember, which in hindsight was so silly because I was Jamaican, but those kids didn't care, or maybe Jamaican booty scratcher just didn't have the same ring. I remember in my first month of class, a classmate told me a curse word and said it meant something good. I wasn't familiar with curse words, so I naturally believed her, until I got pulled aside by the teacher for using this word. I think it was 'fuck' or 'asshole,' I don't remember exactly which one, but I know it was a pretty bad one.

Eventually, I got used to the name calling and the bullying. Well actually, I ignored it and just became a proud teacher's pet. I was smart, hardworking, and loved a new challenge. All my teachers from elementary school to college saw this in me, and I've been a teacher's pet/nerd my whole life.

I wasn't the only one getting used to this new country; I saw my family take jobs that were at the bottom of the barrel, even though they had international experience and degrees. Coming to America as an immigrant is like hitting the reset button, starting all the way over. Nonetheless, my family worked their way from the ground up.

Once my mom found a job in the Bronx, I was reunited with her and my brothers. Our first Bronx apartment together, I remember we had to be extra quiet because the landlord only thought my mom had one child, my at the time, three-year-old brother. When the landlord came upstairs for rent, my middle brother and I had to hide in the closet so that the landlord wouldn't kick us out. After about eight months of this, the landlord found out, and we had to move. We moved to a three-bedroom apartment in a three-family home a few blocks away from where we currently lived. My mother and baby brother shared a room, while my grandmother and uncle shared one, and my two brothers, I and a cousin shared another. It was a squeeze and a hectic household, but this was our lives for around five years. During that time, my mother was able to save up and purchase her own three family home. Worth it? I would say heck yes!

This experience taught me all about delayed gratification. I know my mom didn't want to live that crammed with family but look at the reward! Many families are never able to buy a home. Within 10 years of being in America, my mother was able to do so while being a single mom of three. She taught me how to stretch one dollar to make it feel like twenty, how to use everything you have.

Moving forward to 2010, it was my sophomore year in high school. I was fifteen and ready to take on the world. I had permed my hair for the first time, the summer before 10th grade, and all the boys who wouldn't even look my way before, had all eyes on me. My new straight, long hair had boys whispering sweet nothings in my ears, along with my already daring, very outgoing and friendly personality. Mix that with my newfound freedom and teenage hormones. Oh, I was a force to be reckoned with. I felt I was smart enough to indulge in teen misbehaviors because when it came down to the wire:

I was the most responsible out of my friend group (as quoted by their parents).

I deserved it the most due to my mostly sheltered childhood (in comparison to my friends, I don't have stories of sleepovers, playing on the block in the summer, being told to go play and be back home before the street lights, etc.).

I was a high performing student, and I needed some FUN.

My mom, though, didn't feel my reasoning stood ground. So, naturally, I did what any teenager would do. I did what I wanted. I was skipping school, staying out late, snuck out a few times. I was smoking weed, hanging out with boys, and having a merry 'ol time. That year, I failed my first class ever and was lined up for summer school. My mom tried taking me to therapy, but I objected because "I'm not crazy, why do I need a therapist." She then tried to sneak me to therapy by taking me on a "trip", and I didn't find out it was the therapist's office until we arrived. I was not happy or willing to participate. My mom had enough though at this point.

At the end of the summer, I was to be sent to live with my father in Baldwin, Long Island, as he had recently migrated to the US. Since my dad was now geographically closer, it was his turn to try and figure me out. I wasn't too happy about this. Actually, I was distraught. I loved my dad and his side of the family, but I didn't want to leave my school, my friends, the Bronx! I didn't really have a choice. My bags were packed, and I was gone.

Again, I was in a new place, all alone, having to press the reset button. While in this new environment, I had to adapt and adapt quickly! Baldwin Senior High School was my introduction to affluent black folks. This experience truly opened my eyes to what upper middle class, and even wealthy black people, looked like; what it was like to go to a diverse school with more than Black and Hispanic kids.

Although I hated the idea of moving initially, I did end up loving it and being grateful for being sent there. I'll talk about that more in future chapters.

Let's get back to being Resourceful AF. It was 2011, and I was halfway through my junior year, well assimilated into the Baldwin ecosystem. I had my friend circle, involved in school activities, joined a magazine, and met one of the most influential women in my life (Sharna Jenkins), in those few months. Little did I know that I would soon have to tap into my resourcefulness, while simultaneously making one of the most significant decisions of my life.

Spring break rolled around. Let's say as a 16-year-old, who was finally permitted to go hang out with friends, friends with cars, that spring break I made some not so smart decisions. I partied, and 'Netflix and chilled' more than I should have.

Once back in school in May, I was going about my usual ways when I realized I had missed my period. It was around SAT and ACT time, and I was also applying for colleges, and studying for Regents exams. Naturally, I attributed the missed period to stress, as suggested by my aggressive Google search. Then June came along, and once again, no period. School season was coming to an end, and I was eating pizza every day.

One day I felt super nauseous and thought maybe I had a stomach virus from binge eating pizza for the last two weeks. As if eating the same meal for fourteen days wasn't enough of a sign. I kept feeling like I needed to throw up, but the moment never came. I decided to go to Urgent Care and get checked out. I was in the waiting room for thirty minutes. I went in and did the usual; weight, height, temperature, blood pressure, pee in a cup, and then waited for the doctor to see me. After what felt like an eternity, but was really 10 minutes, the doctor came in and said they were still testing my urine and started questioning me about my symptoms and pain. I explained I kept feeling like I needed to throw up, but nothing comes up. She asked the obvious. "Could you be pregnant?" "What's your sex history," etc., to which I laughed and replied, "Nah, no way. It's just a stomach virus. Viruses have been going around, and I've eaten pizza every day for the past two weeks. Maybe it's the pizza restaurant."

Another reason I was 100% sure I was NOT pregnant was that I took a pregnancy test about two weeks before this doctor's visit. In hindsight, I realize that I'd read it completely wrong.

Anyway, the doctor said okay, left the room to retrieve the urine, and came back in another five minutes. She then sat down and said, "Well, the test is back, and you're pregnant."

I'm going to pause here, because what I did next... Y'all, please don't laugh.

I looked into the woman's eyes and burst out laughing. She stayed straight-faced. When I caught my breath, I proceeded to say, "Really funny, but I just told you I can't be pregnant. I didn't tell you, but I already took a pregnancy test, and it was negative, but I did deserve that joke."

Seriously. This is precisely what my hormone-raging, egotistic 16-year old self said to a doctor with years of medical experience.

With a now serious face, she replied, "It would have been funny, but I'm not joking." My whole heart exited my body through my ass. I was shaking! My mind started racing...Pregnant? WTF? Really Google, you said this was stress. When I have a headache, you tell me how I'm dying of brain cancer, but now when I needed to be more prepared, you had me self-diagnosed with fucking stress? (That was the day I stopped relying solely on Google symptoms.) Really pregnancy test? Why aren't pregnancy tests easier to read? That second line was so faded. Why didn't I just buy the more expensive one that read "pregnant" or "not pregnant".

FUCKKK I'M PREGNANT!!! This isn't even the worst thing the lady said. At this point I was in tears, not the 'sad' tears, but 'fuck my life, I'm about to die' tears, and I couldn't think straight. Her next words were what prompted all tears to stop and here is where my resourcefulness kicked in. She said, "Now I have to call your mother." I said, "No, she can't be called. Can you speak to my Dad?" Mind you, my dad was currently overseas, in Jamaica. So, I had to text him to call this doctor and wait in her office until he called, and she spoke to him. Then I was able to leave the office. My grandmother and her best friend picked me up, and I said not a word to them. I headed to Ms. Jenkins' house, and she was the first person I told.

Side note: That doctor didn't have the right to demand to speak to my parents. Once pregnant, I am legally emancipated/responsible for myself. When I found out that I could have told her no and she couldn't force me to call/tell them, and she could get into trouble once I didn't give her permission because of HIPPA regulations, I was so upset. In hindsight, I realize she was only looking out for me as a pregnant 16-year old black girl. I could have made some terrible decisions if my parents didn't get involved. So, Doc, thanks!

A few weeks later, it was summer, and my body was changing. Not many people knew, besides my close friends and individual family members. My mother didn't find out until the fall when my Dad opted to tell her.

I was about to begin my senior year of high school. I was looking at colleges. I was taking some college credit classes in the Fall, and I had a Summer Enrichment Accounting program. I had to be resourceful and think outside the box. How would I take care of the baby? Would I get kicked out of school? Would I finish on time? Would I go to prom? Well, this book is about getting shit done, and that is precisely what I did.

I completed my summer program and started senior year in the fall. I let the school nurses, guidance counselor, and specific teachers in on my little surprise. They were shocked but overall, very supportive. Everyone else found out once my stomach started poking out of my now XL sized clothing. I was a part of over seven clubs, everything from debate to yearbook, this particular school year. However, I got nothing but A's, completed my college credit courses, and stayed in school until two weeks before giving birth to my healthy, now six-year-old son, Cameron. The guidance counselor suggested going to an alternative school while pregnant, but I didn't want that. I was okay being 'that pregnant girl' because I knew I was on my best behavior and getting shit done.

After I had Cameron, I was out of school for six weeks. I was supposed to have a homeschool teacher for that time, but because of some administrative mix-ups, that didn't happen, but no problem. I went back to school and finished my senior year very strong, made it onto the Dean's Honor Roll, and I launched my first side hustles to fund my prom and after-prom fees. I sold after-prom tickets and designed and sold the senior T-shirts that read 'Kiss Our Class Goodbye.', The 'ass' in 'class' was a different color so it would stand out. I started commissioning design gigs also. I even designed the senior yearbook and class prank.

In June 2012, I walked across that graduation stage with my six-month-old in the stands cheering me on.

I'm resourceful as fuck, and that continued on to college.

I started college that fall of 2012 directly after graduating high school. I told myself that the only way I was going to college was if it was free. And indeed, five years later, that is precisely what happened.

In my senior year of high school, as my acceptance letters started coming in, I was accepted to places like NYIT, St. John's, and Adelphi, but the scholarship amounts did not cover the full tuition. My ideal school was Baruch College because of its popular Accounting program and low prices. Accounting was my first major. I didn't get accepted to Baruch, but I knew that I would re-apply and that their transfer acceptance rate was higher than their freshman acceptance rate. Transfer it was then. I ended up choosing to go to the local college, Nassau Community College. Because of financial aid - TAP and Pell assistance, I would not only get my tuition fully covered, I would also get a stipend refund each semester. I was practically being paid to go to school because I decided to go to a local community college versus a big-name high-priced university. All my other options for college would have put me thousands of dollars in debt.

Let's take another pause to point something else out. My mom sending me away was also a bonus here, because based on her income, I would not have been eligible for this financial aid. But being filed as a dependent on my Dad's taxes, as he made significantly less, made me eligible. So essentially, being kicked out was a blessing in disguise in many ways.

After one and a half years of Nassau Community College and attaining good grades, I reapplied to Baruch, and yes, this time around I did get in! I was set to start in the spring of 2014. Again, with financial aid and with me now filing my own taxes as a young, working single Mom, I was still eligible for TAP and Pell, which meant my entire college career was going to be free.

From the day I was born, resourcefulness was in my DNA. The experiences of my life nurtured that resourcefulness to the point where I'm an extreme problem solver and can think of solutions and create a path where most see none. Being resourceful has saved my ass in many instances, given me access and opportunities in ways that most wouldn't believe or could even imagine. It indeed is one of my strongest traits. I'm grateful for this gift and want to help others tap into their own locked away powers of resourcefulness.

5 Ways to Activate Your Resourcefulness Gene

- Test your limits – put yourself in a situation that makes you have to go above whatever your current limits are.

- Get out of your comfort zone – comfort is nice and fluffy, but it doesn't help you get anything done. Try something new, say hello to strangers, go travel the world.

- Live below your means – if you have less or place yourself within a situation of limited resources, you force yourself to have no choice but to figure out how to maximize the resources you have.

- Attend a hackathon – hackathons are marathon-styled events that bring together community members, educators, entrepreneurs, businesspeople, techies, creatives and more to come up with a solution to a tough problem, all within 24 - 72 hours. It challenges you to think beyond the resources you have while also limiting your time.

- Say yes to doing a task you have no idea how to do – this is pretty self-explanatory, but the reason for it is to put yourself in a situation where you need to 'figure it out'. Just try not to pick something like brain surgery.

BONUS: Ask questions – asking questions allows you to challenge what you know and what you don't know and find out things you didn't know that you didn't know. (Pretty trippy huh?!)

Most often, being resourceful happens in the spur of a moment, but if you are strengthening your resourcefulness muscle little by little each day, then when the time comes for it to be strong, it will be!

CHAPTER 4

JUST DO IT

———∽∽———

> *"Don't reinvent the wheel put rims on it."*
>
> *- Anthony Frasier*

2012 and 2013 were huge "Just Do It" years for me. I had a baby, graduated high school, started college, got my first job, and launched my very first business. Yea, I know, what the heck!

While I was growing up, I always wanted to work so that I could have my own money and do what I wanted with it, aka buy candy, snacks, games, and clothes. My Mom always did her best for us, and my dad sent money from Jamaica when he could, but when all my classmates were rocking Jordans and Nikes, and other cool clothes and shoes, I was subjected to Payless, Marshalls, and JCPenney.

As soon as I turned 14, I went to my school guidance counselor and got my junior work permit. My mother didn't care, I still wasn't allowed to work. She wanted her kids to focus on school. This was super annoying at the time because my friends had jobs working at supermarkets and babysitting (the only jobs that were okay with hiring 14-year-olds). I thought it was so unfair that my mom was stopping me from securing the bag (making money). So, all throughout middle and high school, I never worked. My friends got fast food and retail jobs when they turned 16, and even better ones when they turned 17, but me, I was still not allowed.

Looking back now as an adult, I am happy she didn't allow me to work. Working and going to school is crazy. Yes, the money part seems fun, but not working allowed me to spend my after-school days nerding out in tech. And not being indulged into name brands as a child, allowed me now as an adult, to not go crazy over fancy name brands, but focus on quality "do the job" items. Yass girl, sis is frugal.

Even though I didn't get to have an "official job" in the summer, I would work for my uncle's real estate office when I came for vacation. Then, when I moved to Long Island, I worked for him again and also for my dad's technology repair business. In the summer after high school, I got my first paid internship. It was at a local doctor's office, doing their administrative paperwork, which I was already an expert at from my years in Real Estate. It was a 100-year-old office (actually 30 years), but it smelled like 100. They had not digitized any of their information, and in the middle of 2012, having only paper records was no good. My role was to review files, organize, and then digitize. Yay, fun! Yea, not really, but I was happy to be working.

I was very grateful for my grandmother, who babysat Cameron during the day. This allowed me to work. As the fall was approaching, I knew I needed a new job, something that was more consistent and that I actually enjoyed. It was time for Cameron to attend daycare. So, I quit the doctor's office and went on an aggressive job hunt. I figured working at Roosevelt Field Mall, which was close to my school, would be the smartest thing to do so that I didn't waste time commuting from work to school; also the bus near my house stopped at both the mall and my school. Win, win. Unlike most of my Long Island suburban friends, I didn't know how to drive or have a car. So, the bus or the occasional "ride" from a friend/family member was how I got around.

I would've applied to every store in the mall, but at 17 years old, many places were not interested in hiring anyone under 18. So instead, I applied to every store that would hire a 17-year-old employee. I wasn't hearing back from any of them, so I started calling the stores to follow up on my application. Out of all the places I applied, the one that caught my attention the most was FootLocker, Lady FootLocker to be exact.

Every time I went to the mall, I would stop in and ask for a manager to discuss my application. After three visits and no manager available, I decided to call in ahead of time and ask when a manager would be in, and I was sure to get the manager's name. When they gave me the information I asked for, I made my way to the mall and asked for Annette, the store manager, and Kelly, the assistant manager. They probably thought I was a customer or friend because both appeared from the back of the store after the employee radioed them on the walkie. Annette greeted me then went to the back room to look at my application. She came back, and she said she would schedule an interview for early next week. I took it! The following week, I came with my resume in hand, business casual attire, and was interviewed in front of the store in the mall cafeteria. I was hired on the spot!

She told me to come back in two days to be "on-boarded" and start my training. Years later, Annette told me that the reason I was never called back was that I scored too low on the online assessment, but because I was so persistent, she gave me a chance and interviewed me. She also revealed that I landed the job with the last interview question - Annette asked me to sell her a pen. And boy, did I sell that pen! I explained to her in 30 seconds that this was the best pen on the market because it not only had refillable ink, clean, non-bleed-through technology but would also improve her handwriting. That closed the deal!

Within a few months, I was one of the top performing salespeople in the store and already taking assessments for a promotion. I was promoted to a key holder in six months, that's like an Assistant Assistant Manager. Before I knew it, I had employees working under me who were with the company longer and even older than I was. My personal mission was to get to the top.

Being an employee at FootLocker meant that Cameron's first Christmas was lined with Jordans, cool clothes, and lots of toys. I mean, what did you expect? Not only did I have a job, but I also received a stipend refund check from college for about $2K. I was rich by my 17-year-old standards.

The New Year rolled around. I was doing well in school, loved my job, had childcare, and things felt like they were perfect, that is until my entrepreneurial bug started biting again, and I had the urge to start a business/side hustle.

Since I did a lot of T-shirts in high school, I figured it would make sense to launch a clothing line. That is how the idea for Illicit Mind Clothing was planted inside my brain. I spent the next few months researching and developing the Illicit Mind Clothing line, figuring out how I would source shirts, get them printed, sell them online, etc. It was a clothing line that focused on being different, thinking outside the box, and the trinity of love, power, and respect for yourself and those around you. The first logo was an 'M' with a triangle that had an eye in the middle. Yes, very creative, I know. And no, it's not Illuminati.

I used my now rich income to purchase T-shirts, sweaters, wristbands, and tank tops with the Illicit Mind branding. I also created business cards and a website. Everything was moving along correctly, so perfectly that when a friend of mine invited me to go on a group trip to Disney World, I was financially able to say yes. His mom was a travel agent, and they took an annual group trip with friends and family.

In Fall 2013, I launched Illicit Mind Clothing and reapplied to Baruch College, this time as a transfer student. I was also promoted to the 34th Street location of Lady Foot Locker, which had way more traffic; hence I started making more money.

It seemed like my winning streak started up again. I got the news that I was accepted to Baruch and would start in Spring 2014. It wasn't long before my social media and in-person marketing for the clothing line paid off. I made back my initial investment pretty fast, but I also bought a ton of inventory. So even though I was profiting, I had a ton more product to get sold. Please note, this was 2013, before I learned about drop shipping, so my only option was bulk ordering and keeping inventory on hand. I also got my first apartment in the Bronx because that would have been more convenient for traveling now that I would be working and going to school in Manhattan.

I was getting sh*t done, living my best life, succeeding at almost any challenge I took on.

Here are 10 Strategies to Help You Just Do It

Be proactive

Don't wait for life to force you to make a change. Make that change consciously on your own time.

Use Your Creativity

Think outside the box on how to get something done. We may not see it initially, but you always have everything you need. Your notebook isn't just a notebook it's a prop to use in that video you want to create, your paperclip can transform into a binder wire. So many options and solutions when you think outside the reach of your five senses.

Leave Things and People Who No Longer Serve You

This one is difficult, but being resourceful isn't about using what you have to the best of your capabilities, it's also about getting rid of what you don't need so that it doesn't take up space or negatively impact the things you do have.

Live Below Your Means

No, you don't need those materialistic items. Well, maybe a few. Living below, not just within your means, will teach you that it is never about what you have or don't have, but about what you do with it.

Challenge Yourself

Test yourself. Do something that is super hard, or you have no experience doing. Never back down from a challenge, as there may be something hidden inside for you to learn.

Ask for Help

You won't be able to do it all unless you have supporters and help. Asking for help may seem like you're using other people's resources (time, money attention, etc.) but the fact that you know you don't have those items, you need them, and this other person can provide you with them, shows that you know how to find what you need when you need it.

Pursue Multiple Paths

Having more than one thing going for you at a time will teach you to be resourceful. I suggest two, but never more than three, so you can pace yourself and learn how to manage your limited resources for the best ROI.

Be Persistent

Overnight success most often takes 10 years. Go at a steady pace. Don't give up so easily on things that seem challenging or overbearing.

Stay Positive

Having a view of "this will work out" vs. an "I don't have enough I can't do it" point of view can make all the difference. Self-confidence and a positive attitude can open up doors for you in the real world and also boost your creativity so you can see a path where there previously was none.

Make Widgets Using Thingies

Practice making functioning tools out of random resources. 2012 and 2013 taught me if you want to get something done, just do it. Don't allow your brain to even consider any other option other than getting it done, and get it done by any means necessary.

When I wanted to get a job at Footlocker, I stayed persistent and tried various ways to get in the door.

When I wanted to get into my dream school, I didn't give up when I didn't get accepted. I just created an alternative plan to get to the same destination.

When I wanted to launch a business, I took a look at what I was good at and researched what tools and resources were at my disposal, and just pushed forward my way, makeshift as it was.

None of this was perfect. Sheryl Sandberg said it best, "Done is better than perfect." I got it done! So, can you!

CHAPTER

5

VIRTUOUS MIND

∿

"You can have it all. Just not all at once."

- Oprah Winfrey

Life was good! At least I thought it was...
While I was succeeding professionally in those 2013 months, I was simultaneously mesmerized by my emotionally and mentally abusive boyfriend at the time. His name was Adonis. Everything went entirely south when things got physically abusive.

Adonis seemed like a great guy on the outside, but he had a lot of unsorted emotional baggage, besides his extreme insecurity, which is never the right combination. I should've run for the hills after he made me pay for our first date. Before you judge me, let me explain...

I had a crush on Adonis after seeing him on social media. He was a well-known face on the Bronx party scene. He slid into my DMs and asked me on a date. He didn't seem serious, so the date never happened. One week later, I went to Disney World. Yea, I told you I was rich! With my spring semester refund check plus Illicit Mind sales and working at Foot Locker, I was ballin'.

After I came back from Disney World, I reached out to Adonis in hopes of giving this "date" thing another try. We set a date and time, then met up at this Mexican spot in Manhattan that he suggested.

I didn't order much, this was our first date, and I was kind of nervous. I decided on some tacos and a soda. Adonis, on the other hand, got a fishbowl drink, a Mexican burger, and even a damn dessert. I should've noticed the signs, but I was way too fucking enchanted and excited to be on a date. Why? Most dudes I was interested in were more of "come over and chill", not a whole date. Adonis and I talked, laughed, and had a bunch in common.

Then the bill came. I was low on cash because ya girl balled out in Disney World and all, but I never go on dates or anywhere without being able to cover my travel and meals.

As the bill sat on the table, Adonis looked at the check, and at me, and back at the check. I looked at him, and he looked at me. Then he slowly said, "So you ready to go? Just get the bill." This motherfucker!

I took out my card, placed it on the bill and called the waiter over, mainly because I was confused, but more so to avoid embarrassment. I paid the $82 bill after eating damn near not a fucking thing, and it was time to go. We walked to Times Square and then took the train to his house. Now feel free to judge me. Go ahead. Whatever.

The rest of the summer into the Fall, we embarked on what I thought was an amazing and magical relationship, which ended in the Fall after Adonis slapped the SHIT out of me. Yep, palm to my left cheek. I burst into tears and then apologized to him for getting him mad. He explained that if I didn't laugh and took him more seriously, then it would have never happened. Hours later, he said he was sorry. I spent the night with him like nothing at all had happened. After sharing with a friend what went down, she gave me an ultimatum, "Leave Adonis or we aren't friends anymore." I loved our friendship more than I cared for Adonis, and so I broke up with him. Looking back, it's sad that this is what it took to make me leave, versus having the courage to leave him on my own, but I am forever grateful to that friend.

The next few months after this, my rich, happy life spiraled out of motherfucking control.

In January 2014, I moved to the Bronx to be closer to school and work and finally, live on my own. I had yet to realize the mental hole I was drowning myself in. I was a Mom, working at Foot Locker, and attending Baruch College full time. Let's not forget I had Illicit Mind Clothing to sell and grow.

The months went by, and I thought I was "hanging in there". I tried to make changes like transferring my job from Manhattan to the Bronx to be closer to home and cutting back on hanging out with friends and family to focus on my work. I held photoshoots for Illicit Mind, was in talks with one of my best friends about starting a marketing company and tackling a huge school workload. I thought I could handle the pressure, that I was a strong, black, independent woman. I was superwoman, as many friends and family would refer to me.

However, I was wrong. My load was too heavy, and it was crushing me. I wouldn't say it was the one thing that made me explode, but many small things that I'd ignored led to a full-on blow-up.

By June 2014, I had a 1.7 GPA and on the brink of being kicked out of college and losing my financial aid. I was unemployed and had to apply for food stamps, suffering from anxiety and depression, with two forms of mandatory counseling placed in my fall schedule. Where TF did it all go wrong? It wasn't just one moment, but a series of bad decisions, being burnt out, overwhelmed, and trying to uphold the superwoman syndrome.

Let me break it down for you.

It was 2014, and I had recently moved into my new apartment. I was living in the Bronx with my son and roommates. My roommates were an elderly couple over 60 years old. The husband worked, but the wife was ill and stayed home. There wasn't much correspondence between us. If I saw them, I would say hello or good morning, but I barely ever did. I was excited to start this new part of my life because I had just gotten into my dream school - Baruch College, I had a good job, I was making a path for myself in the NYC startup scene, I was closer to my friends, and finally free to do whatever I wanted as this was my own space. Life was good, at least that's what I thought. The workload of this new school slowly started crushing me, and since I wasn't living at home anymore, I no longer had consistent evening childcare. Cameron had just turned two, but he was in childcare from 7 am – 5 pm daily. With school and work, my days would often not end until 9 pm or 10 pm. I would have to depend on my family and friends to watch him when I had evening classes or worked late. Illicit Mind was also getting a flood of attention. It was as though everything needed me, and my attention and time were being split one thousand ways.

All of this going on at once and I started to get into my head. I felt like a bad mom for not spending enough time with Cameron. I felt like a bad student because I would often fall asleep in class or procrastinate on work. I felt like a bad employee because I was going from being one of the top performing salespeople to not even making it to any lists. I was failing... at everything. This wasn't me. I was supposed to be superwoman, a great student, worker, mom. I tried reading more self-help books, but I couldn't focus long enough to read. I knew there was a problem but didn't have enough time or energy to indeed solve it.

That's when Jesus took the wheel.

It started with panic attacks on the train to work or school. I would start feeling my chest tighten and the train getting smaller and smaller. The NYC subway was already as tight as a can of sardines, add temporary claustrophobia to that, and everything falls apart. My hands would start to shake, my mouth would get dry, and the blood in my body would start racing. A few times I even had to get off the subway and take the bus or walk. As a person who's taken the subway since I was 7 yrs. old, I didn't understand what was going on. Why was I having these attacks?

The worst attack was one that happened at my house.

My middle school ex-boyfriend, Neil, was having some trouble with his current girlfriend and needed a place to crash for the night. I trusted Neil, and the intimate side of our relationship was long over and done with. He had visited before, and we were good friends now. I told him it was okay to crash at my house until the next day. He came over at about midnight. Within 20 minutes, he fell asleep. I was still awake, and my body went into some form of shock. I started shaking, my heart was pumping outside my body, and I felt like I could not breathe or get out of this paralyzed state.

It was not until years later I realized why this happened. I had a long week at work and school, and the pressure of it all came crashing afterward. From the outside, I gave the idea that I was perfect and well put together when in reality, I wasn't. So here I was helping out someone else, and I was the one needing the help. I was on a one-way train to my own demise. It wasn't until an accidental intervention from my college, was I able to come out of this daze for five seconds and honestly see there was a problem, a HUGE freaking problem.

I had to get out of my own head and own way.

My GPA stood at a horrible 1.7, and that meant I wasn't eligible for the accounting program at Baruch Business School, along with the loss of financial aid.

Just like back when I was 16 and found out I was pregnant, and my brain switched into get shit done mode, that was exactly what happened when I got my grades at the end of the semester, along with the email from financial aid stating I would not be receiving any money for school that fall.

I started to seek help. I went to school counselors and administrators to fight my loss of financial aid, and I won, but the win did come with a contract of conditions that I had to abide by. I had to make even more drastic decisions to get my mental health back on track.

- I quit my job at Foot Locker.

- I applied for food stamps.

- I took summer classes.

- I put Illicit Mind Clothing on hold.

And I ordered a print copy of the self-help book, "Choose Yourself" by James Altucher and read it thoroughly.

Within weeks, I was happier, healthier, spending more time with Cameron, doing fantastic in my summer course. I felt grounded within myself. I followed James' suggested daily rituals like writing ten ideas a day, being healthy mentally, physically, emotionally, and spiritually. I picked up a part-time job at Bath and Body Works as well.

I was finally in a good place and every day was getting better.

2014 was the most transformational year of my life. I learned to meditate and finally had someone to talk to who could offer an unbiased opinion and be a listening ear. Thank you, Baruch, for offering therapists to your students. I had one-on-one therapy and group therapy, both of which were a mandatory part of the conditions necessary to get my financial aid.

I started blogging more consistently, sharing my journey and my voice under a blog titled "Virtuous Mind", as a spin-off of Illicit Mind. I was also engaging with James Altucher via Twitter. Every Thursday James held an AMA (ask me anything) session. I, along with many others who read his books and blogs, were always asking questions. I made a name for myself among "The Choose Yourself Community" by being one of the most active AMA question askers.

That fall of 2014, James Altucher was invited to speak at Alley NYC, by a company called The Phat Startup. I was available on the day of the event, and it was free to attend. I thought this would be great! Finally, a chance to meet the guy who wrote the book that helped me change my life.

Alley NYC was right near Times Square, only a train ride away! I got a ticket and was ready to meet James in real life.

The day came, and the event was amazing! I met James and his ex-wife, Claudia. And once I mentioned who I was, they remembered me from Twitter. I was excited and honored, more so I was amazed by this venue and by the company throwing this event. I hung around after the event to try and learn more.

That, ladies and gentlemen, is how I discovered the NYC Tech and Startup scene. Thank you to The Phat Startup team. You opened the door to the next big adventure of my life.

Over the next five months, I attended over fifty tech events, from Digital Dumbo to the monthly NY Tech Meetup. I volunteered for companies like Startup Institute and General Assembly. I also started the Choose Yourself Meetup and Facebook group movement that sparked groups around the world. I read about fifteen books about tech, startups, and entrepreneurship. This showed me that I was not alone. For so long I felt misplaced being a technology-centered, nerdish, entrepreneurial black girl. Diving into the NY Tech Ecosystem showed me there were other tech nerds, entrepreneurs, and people who wanted to get shit done too.

I was now entirely out of my own head and ready to jump back into the world.

Getting out of my own head has been one of the hardest things I've ever had to do. We are our own biggest critics. When someone else compliments and says, "Oh, you did well", what we really think is, "but I could've done great." The constant cycle of not being good enough, doing good enough, or not achieving enough is exhausting. And if it persists too long, it becomes life-threatening. It literally almost killed me.

It wasn't a magic formula or some calculated steps that turned me on the wrong path or that fixed my life. It was baby steps, and signs that led me astray but also that led me back to reality. I realized through these baby steps that I no longer wanted to live in fear of failure and fear of success. I just wanted to be someone and do great things.

Being in my head is one of the reasons why I took so long to write this book. It is why I started this book in 2016, then wrote a substantial chunk in 2017, and now here I am in 2018 finally completing it.

Since I already went through the pain, I want to help you get out of your head or avoid getting in it in the first place.

Five Ways to Get Out of Your Head

- Therapy – Ain't nothing wrong with a little professional help. When I was 15, and my mom suggested therapy I had such a negative view of it. "I'm not crazy, why would I need a therapist." After being enrolled in mandatory therapy at 19, I realized that therapy is there to help me get to the core of whatever problems I'm experiencing, to express myself and thoughts in a safe space, and to have someone to talk to. It's like any other form of healthcare. When we feel physical pain, we go to the doctor. When we experience spiritual pain, we go to church. When we feel emotional pain, we talk to someone we trust, but there is such a taboo on mental pain and seeking a therapist. To this day I continue to see a therapist and I'M PROUD! And I share this very publicly to help remove the stigma about seeking help with mental health. I often imagine how many mistakes I could have avoided if the 15-year-old me was more open to getting that help I needed to manage my emotions and mental health.

- Friends and family – Reach out to those you love and trust, who will give you the emotional support you need to see your greatness!

- Journaling – Write it down and then re-read it. Clogging your mind makes it even harder to see the bigger picture. Also, journaling is a great way to reflect.

- Talk to yourself out loud – When you hear yourself doubting, bring it into perspective where you can kick that negative idea out.

- Facts vs. Fiction – Look at the facts of the topic that you have stuck in your head. Sometimes you will see that what is driving you crazy is more fiction than fact, that you actually can achieve or do the thing you are telling yourself you can't.

Five Reasons to Get Out of Your Own Head

- Happiness – I was so much happier when I wasn't blocking my blessings or settling for less.

- Success – Once I wasn't in my way anymore, success in various areas of my professional and personal life started to pour in.

- Sound Mental Health – If you can think it, you can be it. When all my thoughts were negative and condescending, I was holding myself back. When I overcame those limiting thoughts, I was able to focus my time and energy in the right places.

- Clarity – Being blocked mentally and just living in a blur influenced my unhealthy choices, but once I achieved clarity around who I wanted to be and the things I wanted to do, my vision for my life became so much easier to SEE a bright future was ahead.

- Confidence – HELLO! This speaks for itself. We are our own biggest enemies at times. That led to a lack of confidence and belief in myself that I could be great. Even though others would say it, it wasn't until I said it to myself that I could fully believe it.

Three Consequences of Not Getting Out of Your Head

- Regret – If you don't ever get out of your head, you will have a long list of "what if" and "I could have". They sometimes trail you for the rest of your life. Who wants an ugly list like that following them forever? Not me, and you shouldn't either!

- Detrimental Mental Health – Unlike physical illnesses, you can't see mental illness or your brain crumbling to pieces, which is exactly what happens when you live a life of fear and regret.

Envy – Oh, the green-eyed monster! It will attack when you least expect. Living a life, you don't enjoy will lead you to be envious and jealous of what others have. Please don't be that Guy/Girl.

CHAPTER

6

POWER OF BROKE

~~~

> *"There are no great limits to growth because there are no limits of human intelligence, imagination, and wonder."*
>
> *- Ronald Reagan*

That last chapter of my life was crazy. While writing this, in hindsight, I just want to thank God and say how grateful I am that I made it through that time of my life, because things could have gone a completely different way.

After quitting my job at FootLocker, I had to find a way to pay my bills, food, rent, daycare, phone bill, and cable. That is when I decided to become a part-time stripper. Just kidding, lol. Although this did cross my mind. I found a local gig at the Bath and Body Works close to my house.

I worked there for the summer of 2014, and for the most part, I enjoyed the work, but I just didn't see much growth in it. And if you learned anything about me so far, I need growth to survive. I like to learn and continuously develop.

I was becoming rich with knowledge, connections, joy, self-worth, but when it came to money, I was broke. I was broke as shit.

I quit Bath and Body Works before I started my Fall, 2014 classes. I knew it wouldn't be a good idea to work so far from my school. Also, I was still in my "'repair stage'" and doing too many things at once got me into the mess I was currently in. I started working at the school's Barnes and Noble cafe and in the Admissions office through work-study. After a few weeks in these roles, again, I quit. The cafe was great and all, but I couldn't make the milk foam to save my life. As a non-coffee drinker, I never knew the vital importance of foamed milk in coffee. And the work-study felt like torture. Literally, just like the doctor's office from 2012 with outdated systems that no one wanted to upgrade, they didn't even want to hear my ideas for upgrades. They were stuck in the dark ages, and I was an innovator. My motto is "Let's build, or I'll go bye-bye."

I had my financial aid, savings, and then borrowed from family and friends to make ends meet. I was grateful to receive government benefits, although I felt profoundly embarrassed and judged when I walked into the offices. I felt like everyone would just stare and judge. And the wait times would often have me there for the entire day, literally. Nonetheless, I had a mouth to feed and put any shame and ego I held to the side.

When you're broke your "creative juices" start to bubble instantly. From this, I started a few side hustles to make some money. I created websites for folks using Weebly and Wix. I did small graphic flyers and just odd jobs. There were also my unpaid side hustles that just made my heart warm, like the Choose Yourself community. After many weeks of engaging with other "Choose Yourselfers" on James' AMA, I decided to create a website and Facebook group where I would convene with and engage with other CYers (Choose Yourselfers). I just wanted to learn more about why others choose themselves and if they could use any support, because unlike myself who had help from not one but two forms of therapy while on the journey of accepting myself, I knew that someone out there could use a bit of a booster.

The Facebook group started to grow slowly but surely. James even tweeted about it and joined the group himself. By Early

2015, the group was growing bigger and bigger. At this point, everything had been online through the website and Facebook group. I figured why not have people meet in person? That's when I created the first Choose Yourself Meetup group in NYC and then other Choose Yourself members followed and formed their own local groups. I mean, it spread like wildfire, groups were created in California, Texas, Florida, even internationally in Canada, Australia, and Thailand. I was ecstatic! This small little idea I had was impacting so many people across the world.

I then hosted the very first Choose Yourself Meetup in NYC in March of 2015. We had about fifty people attend. I know you're probably wondering, "How does the broke girl on food stamps, host an event in NYC, catering to 50 people?" Well, that's easy, I used the power of broke. Here's how I did it.

Since I'd been networking in the ecosystem, I asked a couple people that I'd met to be speakers, and also asked to be connected with a venue that could sponsor the event. I locked in four amazing speakers. I even asked my classmates at school to participate and locked in two of them to be motivational speakers doing a group activity, and another who performed a song. Resourceful AF, right! A friend who was an employee of at General Assembly, remembered me from when I volunteered there previously and was able to provide the space free of charge.

Then, there was the matter of food. As mentioned previously, I wasn't making any money with my part-time job, but I did have a food stamps card. This is the first time I'm saying this publicly.

For that very first meetup, I went to BJ's, bought refreshments with my food stamps card, then to the Dollar Store to buy supplies with the money I made via ticket sales. I stayed up all night preparing platters and had a friend drive me from the Bronx 238th Street to 23rd Street in Manhattan that morning for the event. I was late, we had a slightly rough start, but overall, the event was super successful.

After the event, James wrote an article about the group and the Choose Yourself community on LinkedIn. A photo of me leading the event was the article header. I felt so honored and proud. The group took off again after that. The group is still around today, over four years later, with over 10K members.

Being broke allowed me to humble myself, be creative, and think all the way outside the box. I created so much value, connects, and learned so much in the time that I was broke. Being broke allowed me to tap into superpowers I didn't even know I had. That is the Power of Broke!

My creativity increased so much while I was broke. For example, like the time I walked into the bank with $52 worth of coins and walked out with a brand-new Fitbit.

Blog post from Virtuous Mind Blog

Title: Walked into the bank with $52 worth of coins, walked out with a brand-new Fitbit. Here's how:

Originally Published: 2/12/2015

I always find myself in unusual situations where I make good decisions that start out small and then turn into something huge. On Feb 11th, 2015, I walked into TD Bank on 23rd Street and Lexington, carrying all the coins that were once in my son's piggy bank. (We were saying bye-bye to the piggy bank and hello to a bank account, because at 3 years old his piggy was already full).

Once inside I was greeted by a banker named Ashley. I asked her about TD Bank's money counting machine. She responded by letting me know that indeed they do have a coin counter, but there is an 8% fee charged to non-TD members. With my super heavy book bag on my back carrying all $52 worth of quarters, pennies, nickels and dimes I was a little disappointed that my son would lose 8% of his good hard savings.

That's when I asked her the most reasonable question ever. "Does TD offer a free college student bank account?" She responded with a smile and a "Yes."

That was all I needed to hear. I sat down, gave all the necessary information to create my TD account. Ashley even offered me a cup of my favorite tea! (Red Zinger). Within less than 30 minutes I was now a TD Bank client and my son's money would not be subjected to this 8% fee! Win-win.

But then the winning did not stop. Ashley brought me over to use the coin counter. The machine prompted me to "guess" the amount that the coins are worth. Since I counted them the night before I knew they were worth $52. Once the machine counted the money, and my guess was accurate. It told me I was a winner and to claim my prize at the counter! I hope you guys are counting. That's three wins so far!

Now once my card was ready, and my coins were counted Ashley presented me with a TD goody bag!

The bag contained a baseball, water bottle, and a Fitbit!

Oh, the winning just didn't stop!

TD Bank and Ashley offered such excellent customer service. From a friendly warm welcome, to my favorite tea, to setting up my new account, saving me from an 8% fee, helping me redeem my coin and leaving me with a bag full of goodies, it was all too good to be true!!

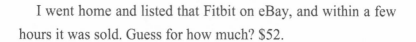

I went home and listed that Fitbit on eBay, and within a few hours it was sold. Guess for how much? $52.

All this from the experiences I had while broke. I decided to write a short eBook called the "40 Benefits of Being Broke". I never published the book though, until now.

Written in 2014

Hey! This is my introduction (but you already knew that). Well hello, world. My name is Georgie-Ann. I am an entrepreneur, 19 years old, a single mom, and a full-time college student. Oh, and yea, I'm broke!

I know this title may have you thinking. What in the world? How can being broke be beneficial in any way? Well, being broke is very helpful in many ways. To be honest, going broke is probably one of the best things to ever happen to me. I will be sharing with you what I have found to be some genuinely awesome benefits of being broke. Forty is just a small number of the benefits that I saw.

Before we get started, I want you to learn how I define being broke.

When something is broke/broken, what do you usually do? Seek help to fix it. Right? Whether it is your mom's brand new vase that you broke while testing if you can walk a straight line with a vase on your head or a leg that was broken because you were roller skating and forgot that you were only a pro roller skater in your past life (yea, that's my version of a joke). Anyways, the equation is simple:

Broke + Assistance Sought = Fixed

The best thing about something that was once broken is that when you do fix it, it is made stronger and decreases the possibilities of it ever breaking again.

What does that have to do with being broke regarding money? Well, the concept of being broke and broken are the same thing. The majority of rich and successful people will tell you that at a time in their lives they were broke. They went from broke to rich based on their individual circumstances. I hope you just asked yourself, "Then where are my riches?" That, my friend, is different based on which rainbow you are chasing.

After you finish this book, hopefully, you'd have seen exactly what I mean because there are unlimited benefits of being broke. Being broke is an elevator to success, but only if you don't follow those people taking the stairs.

The benefits are in no particular order. Seriously, all I did was write out forty benefits on index cards, shuffled them, and then laid them out on the floor, and that's how the order was determined. Some of the benefits have extended examples, while others, well they are a lot shorter. Sometimes you just need to have some fun, do something, and you know, relax.

Oh, and by the way, this is in no way a recommendation to go broke so you can be successful!

Enjoy!

1. *You fall in love more.*

You may want to re-read number one. And no, I'm not crazy, I'm just honest. Being broke allowed me to see and appreciate more of the little things in life, especially being a New Yorker, since New York City has been classified as one of the unhappiest cities in America. Yup, that's New York City for you. Being a New Yorker, you are almost taught it's okay to be angry, rushing, and annoyed at all times. This is why when you slow down, people think, "Wow! This person is crazy, absolutely nuts." When you actually take the time to recognize that you are surrounded by millions of people, that the sun is shining a little brighter than it did yesterday, that the rainwater makes the flowers glisten, that the skyscrapers are beautiful pieces of artwork that took a lot of time and hard work, then you begin to fall in love more. Focusing on money and a job that you dislike, or maybe even hate, makes you miss out on all the opportunities to fall in love. Funnily enough, if you fell in love more, your work ethic, performance, and overall experience would increase.

I started falling in love every second once I was broke. I started seeing small things as large blessings. I would fall in love with something as simple as how today it didn't rain because I currently don't have an umbrella and I didn't want to spend any money on one.

You can do this too. Broke or not, falling in love with the little thing's life has to offer, will just increase your overall quality of life. Go out today, on your way to work, school, church, anything and just count 10 things that you never noticed about life and those around you.

2. You get to know yourself better

Being broke helps you to go inward. This is not to say that you'll "find yourself" or know who you will become and have a future set in stone. It merely means that you will start figuring out who YOU are, what YOU want, and overall, making your OWN decisions. Cluttering your mind with bills, stress, and how to upsell to a customer's experience will only cloud up your perception of who you are (if you ever worked in retail you know what I mean).

Ever since I've been broke and I accepted it mentally, I've been learning who I really am, figuring out all the things that really matter and are important to me. The things that I was worried about when I had money, I now realize, in hindsight, that I didn't even really want these things.

3. People won't ask you for money

This one is exactly what it says. It's just that simple. When you are financially stable, it's as though you become a bank to others. They come right out and hit you with the famous almighty line, "Help me out, you probably don't need it anyway." Something along that line. How do they know the purpose of your hard-earned money?

I had a prospective business partner a few months back. She was having some trouble with her finances and asked me to loan her money to pay a bill. I lent the money as a way we could build trust. To spare you the annoying little details, know that as I write this book, I'm still waiting to be repaid.

I learned that money is sadly an easy way to make or break a relationship, so be careful.

4. You figure out how to spend/make money wisely.

As they say "Mo[re] money Mo[re] problems." That's only the case when you don't know how to properly spend, or in some cases, not to spend your money.

Having less money to work with, somehow my bills are getting paid off faster than they did when I had money to just buy and do whatever I wanted.

I did 2 simple things to learn how to make and spend money more wisely.

The first thing was that I listened more; I listened to myself, my mentors, teachers, etc. A lot of people have some good things to say, and by good, I don't mean sweet, happy things, I mean honest, raw, uncut things that you may not want to hear so you can be honest with yourself.

The second was, I spoke up more. You know when that financially stable friend says, "Hey, let's go to dinner and a movie," and you know you only have $15 to your name until payday. But your mind (your best friend aka worst enemy) says, "I don't want to look broke," and before you can finish thinking about the situation, you've already agreed and you are even adding additional plans to go shopping. Why did you just do that???

There are many ways that you could have stopped this from happening, but I'm only going to share two.

1. You could've offered the option to do a girls' night in. A home-cooked meal and Netflix can be enjoyable.

2. You could've just been honest and said: "I don't feel like going out this weekend."

But then again as, some random person on the internet said, "You can't be old and wise if you were never young and stupid."

5. You realize that being broke is temporary

As Robert Kiyosaki said in "Rich Dad, Poor Dad", "There is a difference between being poor and being broke; Broke is temporary. Poor is eternal." The idea for this book exploded off of that one line. I feel like deep down I already thought of this concept, but seeing it on paper, seeing it pop out at me, just clarified it all.

A lot of people don't recognize the difference; they think being poor is temporary and that being broke and poor is the same. It's not. You are probably already coming up with a thousand people who are currently rich that were all once poor.

Yes, go ahead, do your happy dance, you are right about those people. But compare your list to the billions of people in this world. Yea, your percentage of "exceptions to the rule" is extremely small.

Just look at it like this; anyone who says that they are broke will usually have money or a solution to their problems soon. Those who are poor never honestly get out of poverty. It's because the 'poor' culture and mindset that teaches you to be a good employee and accept what you get (which is another topic "Rich Dad, Poor Dad" talks about), keeps you stuck in a never-ending cycle. Being taught this often keeps them down from seeing the light and the road to financial success.

Hey, you're broke? Well, me too. Now go do something about it.

6. You become safer

How you may ask? What does being broke have to do with being safe?

Very, very simple.

Broke people cannot afford to endanger themselves.

Every individual broke person is different, but it's just the honest truth.

But for all you example lovers, here are a few ways you can be safer:

- You won't bungee jump off of a bridge (you're broke)

- You won't skydive (you're broke)

- You won't drink (you're broke)

- You won't smoke (you're broke)

- You won't get robbed (you're broke)

- You won't be driving because you won't have gas money

The list can go on forever, but you get my drift.

7. You become more motivated

My motivation can be summed up in one little sentence.

I just want to swipe my debit card and not have to check my balance first.

I don't like to attach my motivation to a person, or a thing because that can quickly disappear. I base my motivation on a goal. So, my goal keeps me going.

You may be wondering why I didn't make my son my motivation, but let's say he is that, and I start working toward getting a more significant income. Once my goal is reached, I'll be less motivated to keep pushing because it was based solely on meeting his needs. However, if my motivation is a goal statement, then I am forever motivated to keep creating more money.

8. You have more time for loved ones

Being broke means, you aren't going to fancy parties, dinners, movies, etc. (it would be worthy to note here that I didn't even go to these when I had money lol). Instead, you just settle for staying close to home and figuring out all the fun and free resources. You go to the park, relax with your family, watch a movie at home, etc. It's not like you have a 40-hr per week underemployment job, that even with 40 hours, would not pay your bills in full or on time. Now, do you see being broke isn't that bad? Please don't go and purposely become broke now. That's a silly idea. No, I lied, that's a stupid idea! Remember that broke is temporary so you will have to do something to get out of your "brokeness."

9. You learn how to make money work for you

Ahh, another "Rich Dad, Poor Dad" objective! I was taught growing up, to go to school, get an education, work hard and success will follow (this is also what Poor Dad taught his son). As I got older and entered the workforce, I got a job, worked hard, got proper checks, then I would get bored. I would want or need more, and it just wasn't happening. I had one source of income. If I worked less, then I had less money. If I worked more, I had more money. This pattern was upsetting. Rich Dad taught his sons to make money work for them, to have multiple sources of income. Especially forms of income that you don't require you to physically be there.

It may not be easy for everyone to go out there and create different sources of income immediately, but there are things that we can do that can help us build alternative sources of income.

You can start a newsletter, invest in a startup, buy and sell real estate, stocks, bonds, etc. I'm not a financial wiz, but there's this website that can lead you in the right direction, and that my friend is called Google.

Just don't put your eggs all in one basket. The money is out there, you worked hard for your money, now make it work hard for you.

10. You have more fun

Finally, we're at this significant part of being broke. There are so many things to do for free or at a low expense. In some cases, you even create something new for fun. You start enjoying the simpler things in life. Your perspective shifts and your favorite park is no longer just a place for loud, ruckus behavior; instead, you're now able to enjoy all of nature's beauty - the trees, flowers, air, sun. Now you are having a blast for free.

11. You become more efficient.

There is no excuse to be inefficient if you are broke. What are you so busy doing that you can't at least try to level up? When you have limited financial resources, you are most times operating at your worst. Your confidence is at its lowest, you sometimes keep finding yourself in messy situations with people, creating worse scenarios than the current one. Why do that to yourself?

Be more efficient and effective. Do things on time, with value, with patience, with concentration. After all, you will reap what you sow. Don't plant carrots and expect an apple tree.

Before acting I weigh the marginal utility (overall benefit) of my actions. If the marginal utility is low, then that thing will simply NOT be done.

12. You become rich

I've been telling all my friends that I'm rich. They look at me as though I just left the crazy house. I believe I'm rich because the foundation I'm laying down at the moment for my life will create infinite value. We are born to create, and that's all I want to do, create until the creator no longer exists. In other words, I will create until I die. Creativity leads to mental richness (being happy and fulfilled with yourself), and financial abundance (those nicely designed pieces of paper that we call money).

13. Society becomes a door and not dead-end.

A lot of people fear what others think of them. "Should I wear the blue dress today? No, my crush might not like the blue dress, but my best friend loves blue. She would think this dress is awesome...wait, no too many decisions. Black shirt and jeans it is today again."

Why do we allow our brains to do that to us? It's as if we are enslaved by our minds. That's some really crazy stuff right there. Most people think they control their minds, but they don't understand that their mind controls them. Let's explore this for a sec. How many times this week have you thought about someone that you told yourself you didn't want to think about? Yea, exactly. We are all zombies to our minds. The only way to get freedom is not to control your entire mind (that would suck, you would have to manage your own breathing, and if you forget to breathe you might die). What I recommend is the 60/40 method. You control 60%, and your brain is allowed up to 40%. This way, you won't have to worry too much about breathing or blinking (it would be kind of weird if you didn't blink either).

Once we learn to control most of our brain, we can now make better decisions, and then you can choose to be objective to the societal standards you agree or disagree with. You will wear that blue dress that you decided to buy. Whoever likes or dislikes it, it won't even matter, so long as you love it.

Society's views are no longer a barrier to your decision-making. It's now an open door of endless possibilities. If people want to accept you or deny you, that's really a "them" problem, not yours.

14. You find more mentors

My mentors currently include James Altucher, Claudia Altucher, Robert Kiyosaki, Kamal Ravikant, Oprah Winfrey, Ryan Porter, and much more.

You are probably thinking how did I meet these people. I met them at Barnes and Noble, reading all the books, articles, blogs, newsletters I could, that were written by these great mentors. Meeting them really opened my eyes.

The way they write, you feel as though this is an essential person in your life, sharing stories and advice with you personally. For me, I'm reminded to accept myself, that I matter as much as everyone else, and success is not an overnight thing. It also reminds me to be honest, to create value, stay strong to myself internally and externally. It's a perfect feeling when you find this kind of guidance. There is much more, but each mentor experience is based on each individual.

I hope to meet my mentors in person, but I'm just going to work on that one day at a time.

15. You have more time to DO things

Let's just note that I just wrote a book. If I weren't broke, I would've been too busy overworking for an underpaying job, hoping that one day everything will be fine.

If you have the time, then do things. It doesn't matter what things they are, just as long they benefit you or others, go ahead. Just do it! Create!

16. You have more time to read.

I remember when I was younger, I would tell my mom that I'm bored, and her first recommendation would be "go read a book". As soon as I was told to do that, I didn't waste any time finding something else to do to avoid reading. Now I don't regret the advice because now I see how critical it is. The knowledge and insight I gained by reading books have helped hone my vocabulary and world view.

When you're broke, reading brings you all sorts of knowledge, adventures, ideas, etc.

Books I read this year:

- "Choose Yourself" - James Altucher
- "The Power of No" - James and Claudia Altucher

Reading at this exact moment:

- "Rich Dad, Poor Dad" - Robert Kiyosaki
- "Make your own lunch" - Ryan Porter

Next up to read:

- "7 habits of highly effective people " - Stephen Covey
- "#Girlboss" - Sophia Amoroso

Reading is a great thing! There is a book on every possible topic you can think of, and if you can think of a topic that a book hasn't been written on, then simply write that book!

17. You enjoy abundance

Ahh, abundance! Enjoy it, embrace it, and find the areas in your life that have the most of it.

When I was working, I pretty much forgot all the things that made my life abundant. I was too distracted by what I didn't have or what I was trying to achieve more of. Now I am aware of what I have, and it must not be taken for granted.

18. You can sleep in late

I'm not saying this to be lazy, but after a long week, it's nice to sleep in on a Saturday morning.

Our bodies need rest to re-energize for the adventures to come.

19. You become an idea machine

The 'idea machine' is a term I learned about from James Altucher. The concept is to not only think, but to also write down ten ideas a day. No matter if the ideas are good or bad. Write them down, and each day, follow through with the process. James states that the brain is a muscle, and with every muscle, you must exercise it, or it starts to atrophy (waste away).

20. You strengthen yourself.

Having all this time and freedom, I've gotten the chance to just build myself in many ways.

When I had more money, I would suffer constant panic attacks and stress over bills, worry about everything. I consider myself so weak because of that. There were days I even felt like giving up, throwing in the towel and saying I'm done with all the madness.

With a lot of pressure being lifted off my shoulders, reading, opening up, writing, talking, and much more, I'm now focused on building back my strength to be the real me.

Halfway through, guys. I hope you're not reading this all in one shot. Take a break. Eat some fruit, walk around your house, take a bathroom break!

21. You have more time to take walks.

Living in NYC, when you have a $5 MetroCard for the day, you have a lot of places to explore, and a lot of time to take walks. Walking is fun, easy, and gives you a chance to exercise, breathe, and relax. Try it.

22. You become healthier emotionally

Emotions, aww man. These things will get the best and the worst of a person. When you have less money and more time on your hands you are forced to work on how you feel emotionally.

What make your heart warm and puts a smile on your face. You are jolted into dealing with reality instead of denying it.

23. You become more important

Being broke taught me so much about putting myself first and valuing myself even more. I was now my main priority.

24. You have more good ideas.

Earlier in #19 when I mentioned you become an idea machine, the more ideas you have, the more you will be able to produce. James Altucher also suggests that your ideas have sex and create great idea babies. A great analogy, I guess, is two ugly people (bad ideas) create pretty babies (good ideas).

Take me for example. I had the idea to write 40 benefits I got from being broke. It was apparently a good idea because here you are, reading my book (hope that made you smile).

25. You can get eight hours of sleep every night

You have no reason not to!

26. You eat better

When I didn't have the money to afford lots of different foods, I had to make a conscious choice about what I did actually eat. It ended up being healthier because I had to cook most of my meals and needed them to be healthy and wholesome so that I wouldn't be hungry 2.5 seconds after eating.

27. You get to know others better

With more time on my hands to just be, I also had more time to listen, to focus, to slow down, and get to understand and know others around me.

28. You become healthier mentally

I started to focus on ways to think clearer, be more mindful. When the world forces you to slow down, you get time to feel and just mentally BE.

29. You become healthier physically

All that walking I had to do to get to where I was going because I couldn't afford certain means of transportation.

30. You become a better hustler

I didn't have a choice but to hustle. And I had to do it well. I was going from gig to gig to freelance to small jobs here and there. I had to maximize any financial opportunity I got.

31. You become healthier spiritually

In this period, I started to become more spiritual. Not in the sense of religion, but more so understanding my spirit, recognizing that there was so much out there around me that was greater than I was, but yet it was a part of me, and I was a part of it, then creating peace of mind around that fact.

32. You create more value

Oh, the value! I was showing up, doing, building, impacting, and creating for others in such an authentic and honest way. The amount of value I created was unimaginable.

33. You have more time to enjoy life

When we are busy and consumed with work, school, money and so many aspects of life, it is as though we just exist. When we slow down, look up and realize that there is so much beauty and magic out there, we become alive. At that moment we get to choose if we will continue existing or we will start living. Being broke basically made a choice for me, and it was to live and enjoy the life I was living.

34. Your own value goes up

The more value you are able to create, the more value you have to share!

35. You connect with people who share your same interests

We often don't "see" others even if they are right in front of us. We have so many layers of dust in front of us that it clouds our judgment and understanding. When you realize that being human and connecting with others doesn't take a long time and it feeds not only your mind but also your soul, it makes it easier for you to just say hello, listen, and build relationships you could have never imagined before.

36. You gain more money management skills

I didn't have much money, so what I did with it and how I spent it, had to be extremely calculated.

37. You have fewer bills

What bills? I had to disconnect some services and choose not to indulge in certain things because AINT NO MONEY, IM BROKE!

38. You become more creative

Creativity will skyrocket when you are down to your last $50, and you need to get your hair done, eat for a week, and buy a weekly MetroCard. When you are strapped for anything such as time, resources, money, etc. you have to go into "how can I get this done with just what I have right here right now" mode. I was always resourceful at my core but being broke just made it go into overdrive.

39. You can go out early

You choose, you have the time.

40. You can stay out late

Your time becomes your most valuable asset. Use it wisely.

Being broke taught me a lot about myself, my experiences, and my expectations. What you can learn from my experience and the experiences of others, is that life and the universe will give you signs. If you ignore the signs and just continue on a path that is not in your best interest, then divine action will change the gear for you.

My life was headed down a negative path, and I was ignoring all the signs it sent telling me to stop, pivot, to do anything other than keep going. Then the universe stepped in, took the wheel out of my hands and told me to get in the back seat (yup, I wasn't even allowed to ride shotgun lol). Don't wait for the universe to step in and take full control before you take action on signs that pop up in your life. You know what the signs are, you see them every day. You may dismiss them as coincidence at first, but they will keep coming, and you might even start to think, "No that's not possible, how are all these things just so conveniently happening like magic."

Let me tell you, it's the universe trying to silently help steer you in the right direction. And if you don't redirect by choice, it will redirect for you.

We see this often when someone is on a path, then the craziest, most unsuspecting life change happens to them; they get an illness, lose their job, a death occurs, new life is being created, they get indicted, they lose their life's work, and so much more. That's the universe taking control to get you back to where you are supposed to be, so you can serve your purpose on this earth because we all are here for a reason.

Listen to the signs, make small changes, grow, and serve your purpose.

In the end, the saying, by Doe Zantamata, "One good thing about hitting rock bottom is the only way to go is up" will finally make sense. And for me that's exactly what happened, things began looking up.

CHAPTER 7

DOING SHIT FOR FREE

———— ⌇⌇ ————

> *"Everything sounds like crap until you are in the right mind-set."*
>
> *– Shonda Rhimes*

I was pretty broke throughout 2014, and it continued through the first few years of my entrepreneurial journey, but I didn't let the lack of money stop me from being involved, giving to others, volunteering, and doing shit for free.

When I started attending networking events and tech meetups, I would focus on the free events only. Even twenty- or thirty-five-dollar tickets were too expensive for me at that time. I had to either miss the costly events or find another way to get in. As resourceful as I was, and armed with the power of broke, I, of course, chose the latter option - I was going to find a way in. The fact that I was only nineteen, and most events served alcohol, meant I had to get creative about how to participate and gain access to the ecosystem. That's when I started volunteering and doing shit for free.

Blog post via my Virtuous Mind Blog

Title: Hacking NYC Events that are 21+

Date: 2/18/2015

I've been to fifty events in the past six months.

These events range from general social events to networking events to full-day presentations, hackathons and the list goes on. What most people don't know, is that some of them, I literally had to work my way into. Some encounters included trying to attend one that was sold out, overbooked, or exclusively 21+. But I still got in. How did I do it?

Simple. I asked. Huh? What? Confused yet?

Every week I'd go event searching via Eventbrite, NTYM.org, and digital NYC. I scan all the events that seem exciting or intriguing, then I start sending RSVPs for different ones. It's all fun, and I'm in a happy zone until... Boom! An event is sold out or even worse!!! The event has an open bar; hence attendees need to be 21+. As you may or may not already know, I just turned twenty years old in December. Attending 21+ events was a big issue.

Whenever this happened, I simply hit "contact host" and send an email, something like this:

> *"Hello,*
>
> *My name is Georgie-Ann. I came across your event via [place] (the site I found the event on). I'm very interested in attending this event, but it is (either sold out/21+). Is there any possible way I would still be able to attend? I am open to volunteering.*
>
> *Hope to hear from you soon.*
>
> *Thank you,*
> *Georgie-Ann*

Simple. Clean to the point. Every time I reached out to someone in this manner, I was able to attend the event... as a volunteer! That's okay. Being a volunteer is one of the best possible roles you can have at an event. Especially a networking or social event.

What's the lesson of my story?? Be a volunteer!

Benefits of being a volunteer:

➤ You have access to the event

➤ Your cost to attend the event is free

➤ You are one of the first people most of the other attendees see

➤ You have access to the attendee list

➤ You gain public/social speaking experience

These are just a few. The list is endless!

Be open to options. You can't let simple barriers hold you back. Figure out alternate ways to get what you want or to get to where you want to be.

Every event that I couldn't afford, I emailed the organization asking if they needed help with marketing, set up, check-in, crowd control, or clean up. Guess what? I got into everything. Not only was I getting admission to events that were ten or twenty, but I was also getting access to conferences that cost over one hundred dollars.

Then I came across various newsletters that would raffle off event tickets, most specifically GarysGuide NYC. I was lucky to win tickets to events there as well.

Being a part of the staffing team often not only gave me admission into the events, but access to food, speakers, and the venue. It was a win, win all the way around. People started recognizing my face and calling me the "events girl". Not to mention, I always wore my Illicit Mind shirts or wristbands and was loaded with business cards to give to anyone who wanted to follow up with me.

More importantly, I asked for the business cards of anyone I found interesting and engaging. In 2016, my Illicit Mind interns went through all the business cards I collected, approximately three hundred of them. Yea, I was not playing. Everyone from CEOs to kitchen staff. If I thought you were cool and wanted to keep in contact, I took your card and emailed you within 24 hours.

I didn't do this on purpose. I just adored people and wanted to continue conversations. Now I realize I was creating social capital and investing in my future. More on this in Chapter 11: Network = Net Worth $$.

Doing shit for free in my early days gave me access and opportunities I needed to engage with the tech community. I didn't have to have money to invest in myself and my business, but I did have time, energy, and creativity. This was the foundation that I set unknowingly for the success I see now.

Not to mention how much I learned while doing shit for free and shadowing some of the most significant tech startups on the scene back then.

Looking back, it's mostly my investments in doing things for free that ended up paying off the most! I am talking about paying off more than ten-fold, in ways that I didn't suspect it to or even imagined it would.

In December of 2014, I reached out to a few people I'd met while networking and offered them a special holiday gift. I didn't have the money or lots of resources to help, but I did have time, energy, a computer, and my creativity.

The message I sent was simple:

"Help with Anything. Over the next 48 hours, I am helping people get things done before the new year rolls around. It doesn't matter what it is, reach out and if I can, I will find a way to help you or connect you with someone else who could help."

I got a ton of responses from people. The tasks were so diverse from general research related tasks, to help with digital services like their websites and more. I was so happy to assist, and everyone appreciated the gesture. I wasn't doing it to get anything in return other than just to offer my assistance, but what I received in return, made it even more worthwhile. I was able to get behind the scene of different businesses, their processes, workflows, and much more. In those 48 hours, I was able to learn so much and try some new things that I was clueless about before.

One of the HWA (Help with Anything) requests actually led to a huge payday for me.

I was doing my regular weekly "events to attend search" and came across an event that was happening on Tuesday, September 23rd. The event was called "Get Ready 2 Launch". It was presented by Canon in partnership with Entrepreneur Magazine. Canon was launching a new printer that would be great for startups and entrepreneurs. But that's not what sold me on the event. Barbara Corcoran from Shark Tank was going to be the Keynote speaker. I was on my entrepreneurial high at the time, so to be in the same room as her, was an opportunity not to be missed.

The event was all day from like 9 am to 4 or 5 pm, jam-packed with panels, keynotes, activities, and food. I signed up. I would always arrive at events early or on time to scope out the scene and get a good seat, close to the stage or presenter was my favorite spot. This shouldn't come as a surprise, I told you I've been a lifelong teacher's pet.

At this event, I met some super awesome and unique people who were entrepreneurs and startup founders. Most of them I'm still in contact with today. One of these fantastic people I met was Gabrielle Curione. At the time, she was the founder of a cancer subscription box that sent "care packages" to cancer patients from their friends and family. The product was called "Chemogram". Her story behind this business venture literally made me more excited about what she was offering.

Her story:

Craig and I were just your average college couple at the University of Pittsburgh. First, he graduated in 2011, then I did in 2012. Our careers took us in different directions-but eventually we were both able to settle in Philadelphia together. We took the leap and moved in together in October 2013. We liked yoga, baseball games, and drinking too much on the weekends.

In December 2013, Craig was diagnosed with Hodgkin's Lymphoma. The diagnosis came as a total shock, but with love and support of family and friends Craig has made a full recovery. After six months of biweekly ABVD chemotherapy and 20 days of radiation, he is 100% cancer free!

Being the girlfriend of someone battling cancer was a pretty emotional ride. I was mad, I was upset, I felt guilty when he felt sick. My most common feeling was a sense of urgency. There were so many people in those waiting rooms week after week. All I wanted to be able to do was support all of them. I developed the idea of Chemogram in that very waiting room in the hope that this product can provide extra support to those strong people going through treatment.

A Chemogram is a specially crafted care package that you can order for your loved one, friend or anyone going through chemotherapy. With Chemogram you can send love in a new, vibrant and heartfelt way.

Chemogram hopes to bring a smile to those individuals undergoing treatment with a simple, beautiful and personalized care package.

All I could say was wow! It takes a lot of strength and energy to overcome one's battle with cancer, and the ride can be terrifying. I think what Gabrielle is doing is just sending a piece of comfort to all those that have to battle each day continuously. Sometimes when you have so many negative things going on around you, you just need a small reminder that everything will be okay. That's what I believe her care packages offer. A little piece of "it will be okay".

When I was emailing my HWA's, I made sure to reach out to Gabrielle. It came at the perfect time. She did indeed need help, and it was something I handled, her website! We started emailing back and forth throughout the next month. I created a whole new, fresh website for Chemogram.

Gabrielle loved it so much she sent me a care package and a tip, which both were totally unexpected.

Gabrielle and I met by chance. I reached out to her offering to help by chance. She needed help. Or maybe none of this was by chance, but a higher power at play helping me on my journey. That experience of re-designing the Chemogram site gave me the courage to seek out even more web design gigs. In the next few months, I got over five clients and made around $4K from building and maintaining websites.

Taking a moment to do something for free may feel like a waste of time, like "I should be doing something that will give me a check upon completion." In actuality, doing that free thing, slowing down, being selfless, helping someone, just acting without the expectation of something in return is what you are supposed to be doing at that moment. I gave without any preconceived expectations, and then the universe gave back to me. I reached out to offer my help, and in return, I got more knowledge, experiences, connections and MONEY!

To this day I continue to do my Help with Anything emails. Every year since 2014, between November and December, I shoot out a message on mailing lists and social channels asking friends and strangers alike, "How can I help you?", and each year I get the opportunity to pay it forward and learn so much from the people around me while creating value and making connections.

I think everyone should do an HWA (help with anything) outreach. Reason being, most of the time we need help but are afraid to ask for it. When someone else asks you first how they can help you, it takes the pressure off.

You don't have to do it around the holidays as I do. I challenge you to start today. To reach out to some folks and ask, "Do you need help with anything?" Shoot me an email or message me on social media and tell me how it goes. Also, I am always offering help if YOU need anything, don't hesitate to reach out. No request is too weird or too big. I've helped people with:

- Getting an introduction to someone they really wanted to meet

- Help motivate someone to make a decision

- Launching a business

- Send an apology to a family member

- Just be a listening ear

- Finding a date

- Fixing up a resume

- Break up with a significant other (Yes, seriously)

- Research

- Hosting an event

- Generating ideas

- Finding an employee

- Booking a flight

- And much more

Someone out there needs YOUR help too!

5 Things you can do for FREE today

- Help with anything

- Talk to a Friend

- Volunteer in your community

- Introduce two people

- Listen to someone

CHAPTER 8

CREATE VALUE

---

*"If you really believe in what you're doing, work hard,
take nothing personally and if something blocks one
route, find another. Never give up."*

- Laurie Notaro

I ended the Fall 2014 - Spring 2015 school year on a very positive note. I passed all my classes, I was less stressed, therapy was just what I needed, and things were going very well. I even got to go to Jamaica for my cousin's wedding in April

2015. All sounds well and perfect, right? Well, it would have been if I didn't have to move less than a week after returning from my trip to Jamaica. The crazy part is, I wasn't being evicted because I was broke, it was because of miscommunication and the ignorance of others.

Post from Virtuous Mind Blog

Title: Always Say Thank You

Originally Published: 5/15/2015

Imagine going on vacation to the beautiful island of Jamaica. One week of fun in the sun with your friends and family. Now imagine less than a week after you return home, you get informed that you have 10 days to find a new apartment.

What would you do? Who would you call, would you just cry? Would you be mad?

Well, no need to imagine. This is exactly what happened to me. And I want to share my story with the world. I will explain why this happened and what I did in response.

THE BACK STORY

For the last year and a half, I rented a room in a 3-family home in the Bronx. The setup was simple, easy, and convenient for my son and me. For the first 6 months, we lived on the 1st floor in a 2-bedroom apartment where our roommates were an elderly couple, around 70 years old. In July of last year, we moved to the second floor of the home. The second floor had recently been renovated, and there was a larger room that would be more suitable for us. At that time, we were the only ones who lived on the second floor.

In late August was when our first roommate, Clara arrived. She is a Jamaican woman who immigrated to America to work while her four kids ages 11–19 stayed back in Jamaica. Clara was about 45–48 years old. Since Clara worked as a maid, she had a huge obsession with cleaning regularly. Our interaction though was minimal.

A few weeks after Clara moved in, a second roommate arrived. Her name was Bianca. Bianca was similar to Clara in the sense that she was also a native of Jamaica who immigrated to America to work. Bianca worked Monday through Friday as a home health aide which meant she was only in the apartment on the weekends. She also had many kids who resided in Jamaica, ages 18–36. Bianca herself was around 57–59 years.

Regardless of the age difference, we tried to make things work.

By early October, Clara and Bianca had built a very close friendship. They regularly hung out and did favors for each other. They also started to gang-up against me. This was when all the disputes began. They began to complain and fuss about everything I did. Once the situation was dealt with and dissolved, it would be mere weeks before they sparked another issue. Month after month the arguments turned to verbal abuse.

Nonetheless, I tried to stay strong. These women were out to get me and would do so at any cost.

HOW IT ALL WENT DOWN

From April 8th to 15th, I was at my beautiful home island of Jamaica for a family wedding. Once back home, I didn't have much interaction with my roommates until the weekend. On Sunday, April 18th, a few of my friends came over to help me make lasagna for dinner. My roommates weren't using the kitchen, so three of my friends were in the kitchen with me chatting and cooking. About an hour went by, and as we were finishing up the dinner, the drama started.

My roommate, Clara, came to the kitchen and gave dirty looks to my friends. Then she yelled out, "I NEED SPACE." I didn't respond to her, and neither did my friends. I just looked at them, and we spoke with our eyes. One person left the kitchen and the other two made some space for her.

Moments later, Clara went to Bianca's room, and Bianca accompanied her back to the kitchen. Bianca also gave dirty looks to my two friends in the kitchen. Then she yelled, "GEORGIE, YOU CAN'T TELL YOUR FRIENDS TO GET OUT THE KITCHEN CAUSE THEY MUST NOT SEE PEOPLE WANT TO USE THE KITCHEN." Once again, I didn't respond. I gave my friends a look, and they understood our unspoken language. My two remaining friends began preparing to exit the kitchen.

I stayed in the kitchen to finish up the fried chicken that was being made to go with the Lasagna. Bianca then went to the sink and aggressively started to wash her dishes. Due to how close the sink was to the stove; water began to splash up from the sink and fall into the pot of hot oil I was using for the fried chicken. I looked at Bianca and said, "Hey Bianca, the water is splashing into the oil, and it's popping up." She immediately went on the attack, turned to me, and yelled, "SHUT THE FUCK UP, GEORGIE!"

My two friends, who were on their way to my bedroom, made a complete turnaround and walked back into the kitchen. I didn't respond to Bianca's disrespectful comments, but my friends felt the need to jump in and stand up for me. They responded to Bianca by stating, "You didn't have to talk to her like that." Bianca then became enraged and started yelling more profanities and marching up and down the apartment. Clara then jumped in making comments that she would call the cops because my friends had no right to be in the apartment because they weren't tenants.

I reached out to my friends, thanked them for defending me, and told them that I didn't need their help. I knew all too well that this was just another angry attempt from Bianca and Clara to bully me, as well as cause chaos in the apartment.

Clara and Bianca continued to yell and disrespect my friends and me for another 30 minutes. They also went on to call the cops and our landlord.

ABOUT AN HOUR LATER

The landlord arrived at the same time as the cops and he was able to speak to them and tell them he would handle the dispute between the tenants. Upon entering the apartment, he demanded that all my friends leave (they wanted to go earlier, but I asked them to stay as witnesses, and also because I didn't feel safe or comfortable to be alone with my son alongside these two monsters in the apartment).

After they left, I was told I was no longer allowed to have friends over. I would like to remind you I was a rent-paying tenant in this apartment and my rent was paid up in full. Without getting to share my side of the story on what really happened, the conversation was over.

THE MOMENT OF TEARS

The following night, my best friend who was also there on Sunday, came over to do my hair. Because of all the madness that occurred the previous night, I made sure we were extra quiet and that she came over when my roommates were sleeping.

Well, at least I thought they were sleeping.

On Tuesday, April 21st around 11 am, I received a call from my landlord. He informed me that I would need to pack my belongings and that I had to leave the apartment. His reason - I didn't follow his rules and that I had someone over after he told me that I was not allowed.

(In connecting the dots of how he knew that I had someone over, was that Clara was still awake and purposely made a complaint to the landlord in efforts to finish the plan she and Bianca sketched out to get me to leave the apartment).

MY FIRST RESPONSE

At first, I was mad that these women had finally got their wish. I was also mad that after all was said and done, I was the one whose life was turned upside down, not theirs. I was also sad because finals were a couple of weeks away, my son was in school, and I couldn't envision how I would find a new place in a hurry.

For about two hours my emotions took over, and I lost it. I couldn't think, focus, or breathe.

HUSTLE MODE KICKED IN

I realized that being emotional wasn't going to help me find a solution to this problem. I had to become proactive. What did I do next?

Step 1: I reached out to my entire network and shared my story. I was asking for ideas and suggestions on what to do to find an apartment.

Step 2: Once the advice started rolling in, I had to sort through them all to see what would work vs. what wouldn't be beneficial at the moment.

Step 3: TURN PLANS INTO ACTIONS. After compiling all the best ideas from my network's feedback, I implemented them. The first one was to start a GoFundMe campaign, the second was to build websites to bring in some fast cash. The third was to reach out to realtors and churches for help.

Results: The GoFundMe campaign raised a total of $1,788. Doing websites got me a total revenue of $500. By searching realtors, I was able to view five apartments that were unfortunately too pricey, too small, or didn't want kids in the apartment.

THE "HAPPILY EVER AFTER"

On Thursday, April 23rd, a close friend informed me about an available unit in her apartment building. This was excellent news until I remembered she lived in New Jersey. I have never been to New Jersey before, much less to just move from New York to New Jersey so suddenly. I still took up her offer to view it on the following day (Friday, April 24th).

I viewed the apartment on Friday, and it was pretty much exactly what I was looking for! I spoke to the manager and told him that I would be back on Monday and that I wanted the apartment.

Long story short, by Monday, April 27th, thanks to the help of my Aunty Yvonne, the apartment was mine. I immediately went back to my previous home and started packing. With the help of friends and family, I got a U-Haul and moved all my stuff to the new location on April 30th. By the following day, I handed in my old keys, took a last look at the place I called home for the previous year and a half. Before I walked out the door, however, I placed two Thank You cards on the kitchen table addressed to my past roommates.

Both cards read:

"Without all your hard work and help I wouldn't have been so encouraged to move out and get my very own apartment. For that, I would like to send you many thanks!! And wish you luck in your future endeavors."

As of May 1st, my old home was just now a chapter in my book of adventures. I am currently bunking at my mom's house until my son and I finish school and get furniture for our new place.

LESSON LEARNED

Life will always throw bricks at you, but you have to catch those bricks and flip them!

I was so grateful for all the family, friends, and even strangers that donated to my campaign. They saw the value in me. Most people left comments about how I'd helped them before, and they were grateful for the chance to help me. I felt so warm by this experience that could have turned my life on its head some more.

Back in the tech ecosystem, I was attending events, connecting, learning, and hosting my own Choose Yourself Meetup events. Around this time, I also started a second group called "Caribbean's in Tech and Entrepreneurship". The same way I felt there was a need to connect the people who wanted to choose themselves, hence, creating the Choose Yourself network, I also thought it was essential to connect and build the Caribbean's In Tech economy. I saw groups like Black in Tech and Latinos in Tech and felt that a Caribbean's in Tech would be just as vital. As Caribbean's, we offer a specific cultural and historical heritage that greatly impacts our technological and entrepreneurial journey. We will talk more about this group a bit more in Chapter 9: Show Up.

Throughout the school year, I was participating in the on-campus Baruch College Entrepreneurship lab, sharing my event attending and producing journeys with them, telling them about the Choose Yourself Facebook group and meetup, and all the things I was doing to become a better entrepreneur.

The team from Lab suggested that I apply for the third cohort of the CSE (Cuny Center for Student Entrepreneurship) incubator that would be taking place in fall 2015. I didn't think I would get in because the only business I had at the time was Illicit Mind. That was a clothing line, not a big entrepreneurial tech venture like the other past graduates from the program. I just had a hobby of connecting people and talking to them.

With that seed freshly planted in my brain to apply, I started thinking about my response of "only having a clothing line." I went home that weekend and asked myself:

Could this be more than a clothing line?

Could Illicit Mind be something more, something bigger?

What is that bigger purpose?

I reflected for hours on the meaning and original purpose of Illicit Mind. Which was:

Illicit Mind is a clothing line that focuses on being different, thinking outside the box, and the trinity of love, power, and respect for yourself and those around you.

Once I said that out loud, it all clicked. Illicit Mind is more, it's meant to be more, and it will be more. I started drafting up a business plan for Illicit Mind that focused on Illicit Mind being a creator of communities and networks, both in person and online. The mission evolved into focusing on the exchange of knowledge, connections, and experiences between individuals. I didn't have a plan to monetize, other than charging ticket sales for specific events or getting sponsors. I knew I loved what I was doing, and each day, I could see the impact and difference I was making for people's lives with the networks I was building. At the foundation of it all, I didn't really care if I was making money, because I was creating value.

With my new trajectory for Illicit Mind, I took a leap of faith and applied to the CSE Incubator.

On May 22nd, 2015 at 10:46 am, I got an email from the CUNY CSE team:

Congratulations! You have been invited to pitch your business to be considered for the Fall 2015 Incubator Cohort.

We will conduct interviews on Wednesday, May 27 from 9am-11am at Baruch College - Newman Vertical Campus Building - 55 Lexington Avenue, in the Field Center, Room 2-140. You will have four minutes to present your business concept and five minutes for Q&A with the judges.

Please email me back with a timeslot of your choice as soon as possible. This is first come, first serve for time slot selection. Once I receive all the responses, I will email you a confirmation with your timeslot and presentation guidelines/FAQs.

By 11 am, I replied selecting the 10:30 am slot.

A few weeks later, it was confirmed that I would be in the Fall 2015 Cohort. CSE received over 100 applications, and somehow, I was selected! Less than a month after feeling like I'd been given a severe blow after being kicked out of my apartment, I was now celebrating a massive win by being accepted into the Incubator.

The incubator program would take place from August to December 2015. I would have to do this program alongside my regular classes, and unfortunately, I wouldn't get school credit. What I would get though, was access to their curriculum, mentors, field trips to tech companies and startups, a stipend of $2,500 per milestone, and a chance to win thousands of dollars at the final demo pitch day in December.

Between May and December of 2015, I became a value-creating machine. I continued my work in various networking groups and circles and was invited to participate in a mastermind group with some of my new friends. We named the group Superhero Mastermind. We met bi-weekly and had accountability partners. After this experience and learning about mastermind and accountability groups, I connected the dots and realized it's what I was doing with the groups I was creating.

I started to focus on building out systems to maintain and grow these groups. Systems that included rules of how to participate in the community, getting volunteer team members to handle crowd control, event organization, digital management, and more.

Once I built this out for the Choose Yourself network, and it started running itself smoothly without much interaction from me, I stepped away from the group a bit to focus more on Illicit Mind. Even though I loved the Choose Yourself community, I knew that it belonged to the people and not to me. This community was for the people, by the people. I was just a tool being used by the universe to set the foundation.

Under Illicit Mind's new business model, I created a few programs. This included:

- Caribbean's in Tech and Entrepreneurship

- Hustlecademy - Classes and workshops to teach innovation in a non-traditional way

- She's A Badass - An event series and community for female entrepreneurs

- Be-Tech - A hackathon series that focused on solving social impact-based issues that would use technology for the betterment of mankind.

- Starter Pack - A creative branding and consulting agency for early stage startups

- Misc. - This was for events that were centered around the Arts

Yea, I was doing a LOT! I was moving at the speed of light, and I didn't want to slow down. My passion for it all made every day, a day to wake up and go harder than I did the day before. I was on cloud nine. I could feel in my soul this was my purpose, my life's work, and to find it while still in college was just wow. I thought, how lucky am I?

Don't get it confused though. At this time, I wasn't making any money. If I did make a few dollars, it would be from Starter

Pack gigs or other miscellaneous freelance things I was doing. I would charge ticket sales for some events and programming, which pretty much just covered the event-related expenses, but most were free. I racked up a little debt during this time but thank God I was still getting financial aid refund checks from school and the stipends from the CSE Incubator were also a huge help.

How was I able to stay afloat while things were speeding? How did I avoid burnout and sinking back into depression? Well, this time around I knew the signs and could act fast when I saw myself headed toward burn out. Taking four classes and participating in the CSE incubator at the same time was too much of a workload for me. I dropped two classes. I knew it was better to pass 2 than fail 4. I also wasn't alone this time around, I was still seeing my therapist, and I had various support systems in school, at home, family & friends, and through the work that I did. The value I was creating had love and support pouring in from every angle.

Back in August 2015, another huge life change happened. I got engaged to my now husband, Bryan. We had only dated for a few weeks before getting engaged. Our relationship was moving pretty fast, but there was something there between us; some kind of larger force and action at play that I just couldn't say no to or ignore. Even with the warnings of "slow down" and "think about this" from my friends and family, I just felt this was right. He was cute, kind, loving, smart, driven, hard-working, and on a 'success' mission. I wasn't the best dressed, so I can't say 'he matched my fly', but he sure did match my ambition, and that was essential.

Attending the CSE incubator, I was learning all these new things about launching a business, setting up a company, systems to maintain a company's professionalism, and balancing business finances. When Bryan got into a dispute with his employer at the time and decided it was time to step out on his own and start his own moving company, I was right there to offer my business expertise and serve as the company's Operations person. He created a plan to get a truck and set up the business profile so we could start getting referral clients through a U-Haul system. I handled the incorporation, tax info, website, business card, and designed some work shirts. In a few weeks, in late October, the business was all ready to go.

In November, he moved into my New Jersey studio with Cameron and me. It was a tight squeeze for the three of us, but we knew this was just a temporary steppingstone for the future we were building together.

December came, and the moving company was doing well. I passed my two classes, and CSE Demo day was approaching. Out of the sixteen companies that got into the program, there were only four remaining, and Illicit Mind was one. Companies got asked to leave for not meeting milestones while others departed on their own for various reasons.

Demo day rolled around, and I placed 4th and received a $3K check. I was so proud, not because of the money, but because of the entire experience and the doors that it opened for me. Just a few months ago, I was on the brink of not applying to this program because I told myself "I only have a clothing line". After this experience, people were calling my work "Ed-Tech" and "Network Building."

Through a CSE mentor, I was also invited to participate in a female college entrepreneurship leadership program called Legacy Out Loud.

I was just doing what I loved and what made me happy. Not only was I creating value for others, but others were seeing the value I had to share.

3 Benefits of Creating Value

1. Everybody Wins - while I was doing what I loved, I simultaneously created experiences, connections, and knowledge for others. I was winning as much as they were. This work didn't drain me, it drove me. And it helped others win. Everybody won! Money is great, don't get me wrong, but after that money is gone you have to ask yourself; what value remains?

2. Your Net Worth Increases - I didn't know this back then, but the value I created lived on and still continues to repay me in various ways. My financial net worth is not

significantly higher if I am still broke, but the value that my expertise brings to the table of having people working with me, connecting with me, is much higher than those around me.

3. People will remember you - to this day, I still get the occasional random message from someone thanking me for HWA tasks that I did years ago. Things I don't even remember doing. Just the fact that I created some lasting value and memory for this person, keeps me in their mind even years later.

Create value! You got this, and you're worth it all.

CHAPTER 9

SHOW UP

—~~~—

"How we spend our days is, of course, how we spend our lives. What we do with this hour, and that one, is what we are doing. A schedule defends from chaos and whim. It is a net for catching days. It is a scaffolding on which a worker can stand and labor with both hands at sections of time. A schedule is a mock-up of reason and order—willed, faked, and so brought into being; it is a peace and a haven set into the wreck of time; it is a lifeboat on which you find

> *yourself, decades later, still living."*
> *- Annie Dillard, The Writing Life*

I believe that showing up is one of the most important things anyone can do for others. Even if you can't bring the person a gift or do much for them beyond being physically present, it truly counts.

When I started attending events in 2014, the key to my success was showing up. Having the gift of resourcefulness plus the power of broke driving my ambition, I didn't only show up, I showed up and stayed present.

I listened, asked questions, gave suggestions (sometimes unsolicited). I became a presence at the events I went to and the communities I belonged to. People saw, heard, and experienced the "Georgie" effect everywhere I went.

I didn't do this to make a statement, I was just used to being the new girl or the misfit. I was used to being an extrovert. I wasn't an extrovert in the "steal your shine" kind of way, but in the "I was paying attention, and I value you kind of way."

When I attended events, and they would talk about topics I didn't understand, I would write down thoughtful questions and ask them during the Q & A portion. When others were fearful of participating in activities where the host said, "Okay we need a few volunteers," I raised my hand and volunteered. A part of me felt like I didn't belong in these rooms, so since I was already there, I might as well learn as much as I can. I always believed in the saying, "closed mouths don't get fed", and I was hungry. Hungry for knowledge, hungry for experiences, hungry for connection, and hungry for success.

This art of showing up and being present started opening up doors for me that I never expected.

It was September 12th, 2014, and the Phat Startup was having an event in NYC featuring James Altucher. I arrived early and met some amazing people in the pre-event mingle. When it was time to take our seats, I sat next to Rondell Anderson of Nothing Short of Greatness (NSOG) who I met earlier in the event mingle. At one point, Anthony Frasier, a cofounder from the Phat Startup, was interviewing James on stage and he stated, "We're going to do some quick pitches for James, who would like to volunteer to come up?"

Rondell encouraged me to go up and give a pitch. I was nervous as hell, but I went up with about ten other people. In the line was another young lady who looked as nervous as I did. Once she hit the stage, her nervousness instantly disappeared. Not only was she no longer nervous, but she also blew away the audience with her pitch.

Wondering what this young lady said to the crowd? She told us that she was a professional Bridesmaid. Yes! I said it right.

She was someone you could hire to be there next to you supporting you the whole time on one of the most important days of your life.

How did it all start? To summarize, Jen Glantz was a bridesmaid four times in one year and had learned all the ins and outs of being a bridesmaid. Not to mention that she really enjoyed being a bridesmaid. One night she posted a listing on craigslist "Professional Bridesmaid for Hire" and within hours her inbox was overflowing with messages! The rest is history.

Hearing Jen speak about her entrepreneurial venture made me think of a few things. Why didn't I think of this? Would anyone want a best friend for hire? Why didn't I hear about her until today?

I went up and gave a quick pitch about Illicit Mind Clothing and the goal to help people think outside the box.

After the event was over, I stayed around to get a photo with James, get Jen's contact info, and meet the Phat Startup team.

In the moments of that event, showing up, participating, and creating value, I was yet to realize the foundations I was setting.

For the first Choose Yourself Meetup event in 2015, James sent us 100 copies of his new book, "Choose Yourself Guide to Wealth". Anthony was one of the panelists who spoke at the event. He also helped me to figure out how to put together and market the event.

A few months later, I volunteered at an event that Rondell produced and I got to meet ET the hip-hop Preacher, the motivational speaker and coach; author and creative, Alex Elle; artist, Marcus Prime; and author, Rob Hill Sr. This exposure to these innovative, impactful entrepreneurs who were also black, gave me a huge boost of confidence while learning the inner workings of event production.

Jen and I stayed in contact, and up to now, she has spoken at various events that I've produced. It was her words this past summer, via Facebook Live, that made me realize why I was having such a hard time finishing this book and gave me the clarity needed to complete the book.

In this quick Facebook Live session, someone asked, "How did you know you needed to write the book? How did you know you needed to share this story?"

Jen responded by saying, "A lot of times we have stories in our lives that we want to share, and we are excited to share. I think you have to be ready. And I think you know you're ready when you have fully told yourself the story again and again and again, over and over again...Especially when it comes to non-fiction. I think it's really hard because we rush to share our story sometimes when they're not ready. People always tell me in my life, you can't write about something you're not over. So, if you're currently going through something, it's always best to wait a little bit of time before you share it with the world."

At this point, I realized that I was still going through the story I wanted to share, that it was a great story, but it just wasn't ready to be shared yet.

Just showing up to that one event opened so many opportunities. Each time I show up, more opportunities come my way.

Show up, be present, do the work, ask the question, and just listen.

5 Simple Yet Highly Effective Ways to Show up

1. Physically - your physical presence in a space where you were asked to or invited to be, can make all the difference to the other person that you are showing up for. Your friend is doing a theater show and invites you, don't flake on them. Show up! They just want to see a familiar face in what may be an ocean of strangers.

2. Mentally - thinking of someone and showing up mentally can have great benefits. For example, you're working at a store and a frequent customer asks you a question, going the extra mile to find the answer and providing them with it shows, "I was thinking of you." That small gesture can lead to unknown forms of future benefits.

3. Emotionally - when someone is struggling emotionally, you just being there, helping them maneuver through that emotion and showing that you care, helps a lot. Asking

them how they are doing, how can you help, if they are okay, can make a world of difference in their lives.

4. By Listening - I remember at many events I would attend, my interaction with people felt so transactional. People just wanted to hand someone their business card and move on to the next person, and if you ask these same people what someone said, you'll find out they weren't listening. We can do better by listening to each other. There is much we can learn. Sometimes we don't even have to say anything, just listen.

Through Conversation - ask questions. When you are somewhere, and they open it up for a Q&A, it's because the hosts want to have a conversation to hear feedback and to interact with the audience. If you think it's awkward being in the audience, imagine what it feels like to be on the stage in front of everyone, and they're not responding. Pretty shitty and scary I would say!

CHAPTER

GOOGLE THAT SHIT

"I wanted you to know that it's perfectly OK and perfectly normal to not know the answer to either of those questions. It's OK to take some time to figure yourself out and explore the many different paths that will lead you to the answers you're looking for."

- Ryan Porter, Make Your Own Lunch

A lot of people have this weird assumption that I'm super smart and just know everything. I want to start off by saying I'm not. Well, I'm not SUPER smart, but I am smart with the ability to be resourceful and a lot of "openness to new knowledge".

Google has been my best friend for as long as it's been around. Before I ask someone the answer to a question, I'll google it first. Most people don't have this natural intuition, and I may not have developed it either if it wasn't for my mother.

When I was growing up, every time I had homework, specifically reading or writing, and I would ask my mom to spell or define a word that I was unsure about, her instant answer was, "Go look it up in the dictionary." Two things you could always find in our home were dictionaries and bibles.

So here I was, a 9-year-old Georgie, unsure of what something like intuition meant and couldn't use the context clues to figure it out, I had no choice but to research it. As the years went by and we got a computer, and the internet was a more accessible, I started doing Yahoo and AOL searches to define words vs. looking in the dictionary. I would also visit websites like Ask Jeeves to figure things out. I knew that if I asked my mom, she would say, "look it up."

From these humble beginnings, I became a look it up, EXPERT! A Problem-solving, everything is figure-it-out-able extraordinaire.

This blessing also doubled as a curse. I became the go-to person to ask about things in my family and friend groups, especially when it came to the use of or interaction with technology. It was as though I created my own version of Ask Jeeves, but instead, it was "Ask Georgie". Everyone wanted help and answers, and they wanted it instantly. They didn't want to search through pages and pages of google search. They expected me to do all that research and data collecting for them then just come to the table with results and answers. For a long time, that's exactly what I did.

- How does this camera work...Ask Georgie

- The VCR is broken...Ask Georgie

- How do I use this international phone calling card...Ask Georgie

- A flight needed to be booked...Ask Georgie

- Laptop needed to be bought...Ask Georgie

- My tv needs to be set up...Ask Georgie

I was tech support, geek squad, ask Jeeves, google search.... You name it! Packaged into a nice melanin "never says no package".

Even though when I was young, I would often get annoyed with people asking me questions they could easily google, it got even more annoying when those same people were now magically gurus on Facebook and Instagram, but still asking me questions like "How do I block someone on Facebook?" Seriously? There's a help center...LOOK IT UP.

I've learned now that many people don't have the first instinct to do research.

My childhood look it up days taught me three key things:

1. I don't know it all

2. Research helps me to learn more

3. I love to learn

The majority of my adulthood has been about learning new things, unlearning old things, and realizing that there are things that I don't even know that I don't know.

Googling that Shit doesn't only teach me things directly, it has allowed me to take advantage of opportunities that I would have never been eligible for.

It all started with the days when I would participate in James Altucher's weekly Twitter #AMA. Not only would I ask questions, but I would also sometimes answer questions that were asked to James. He would answer as many as he could with hundreds of people pitching questions, but I took the authority upon myself to answer some of them for him. From doing that, I started to be seen as a mini thought leader and people would begin to ask me questions directly. If I knew the answer, I would give my best. If I didn't, I looked it up. Through these sessions, I learned about the website Quora, where it was all about people asking and answering questions. I made my way over there and started to build up my "figure it out" muscle even more.

I made it my daily duty to seek out information instead of waiting for the information to come to me. To be proactive about learning, I was reading a bunch of books, creating small research projects for myself online, teaching myself more about graphic design and code.

Then the ultimate challenge came, people started to ask me about doing jobs and gigs I had no idea how to do. What did I do before giving them an answer? I would google it to see if I could learn what to do. Sometimes I would say yes then google that shit later. YouTube and Google became my best friends, then I advanced to Lynda, Coursera, Udacity, and a few other platforms as well.

I was determined to Google that Shit and get the answers I was looking for.

If you take away one thing from this chapter, I hope it is ask and you shall get an answer. There is no such thing as a stupid question. There is so much out there for us to learn that starts with asking questions, answering questions, and Googling the hell out of things.

How to properly google in 4 easy steps

Step 1: Go to Google.com. Your browser may even do an auto google search if you just type the question in the search bar

Step 2: Enter your search terms, type in what you are looking for. It doesn't matter what it is, Google is a smart search engine.

In the case where it doesn't understand your request, it will give you a suggestion of how to better ask that question and get better results.

Step 3: Review your search results. Look at the various links filled with information that Google provides you. Start clicking through them one by one. Ideally, open them in a new tab so you can reference back the search results

Step 4: Refine your search or... go to the next page. Yes, for folks in the back, google has multiple pages.

Google is your friend, well that is if you let it be.

11

NETWORK = NET WORTH $$

"One of the most powerful survival mechanisms is to be part of a tribe, to contribute to a group of like-minded people."

- Seth Godin

We have all heard the saying your Network = your Net worth. It simply means who you know will affect the amount you can earn financially throughout your lifetime. We see this proven every day when millionaires and billionaires increase the Net worth of the people they know through partnerships and introductions.

That leaves us with the questions:

1. How do I organically build these networks?

2. Can I make valuable connections if I'm not born into an already wealthy circle?

I can say firsthand from my years being an entrepreneur and freelancer, that the networks I've built and been a part of, have directly impacted my financial earnings. The people I met allowed me to gain more connections, and experiences. From those experiences, I gained more knowledge, created value, showed up, and got shit done. All of the actions that I once thought were random, started to add up and make sense.

Your Network is your Net Worth!!

It was January 2016 and time to go full on GRIND mode. I was ready to take the new Illicit Mind into the world and make a name for ourselves. The CSE Incubator was over, and we were no longer Illicit Mind Clothing but instead now, Illicit Mind Inc. – a membership-based tribe of young adults learning and communicating through a series of entrepreneurial and technology-centered events.

I had planned one to two events per month for the next six months. I was running around like a chicken with no head. I built and managed the website, marketing materials, social media, sourced venues, speakers, figured out food options, sponsors, I did everything. I was actively looking for team members. I had friends and colleagues that would often offer support, whether it was volunteering to help with my events or sharing my work online.

During college Winter Break, that January, I hired my first three interns, Sidni, Shellie, and Cassandra. They were amazing! They helped me to organize, strategize, and plan for Illicit Mind. It felt great to not have to be the jack of all trades. Illicit Mind wasn't turning a profit so I couldn't pay them, but I did cover meals and transportation. After our month together, they had to head back to school to start the spring 2016 semester. I was sad they had to leave, but proud that I was able to work with and mentor these girls, who like me, were black and interested in technology and entrepreneurship.

Spring 2016, things were steady with Illicit Mind events. I partnered with a Baruch Alum that I'd met at a hackathon in December. He had attended my February hackathon, and we started discussing working together on a Fintech hackathon that would focus on solving issues in our community. We recognized that we were part of a small group of early adopters who knew about things like hackathons and the tech ecosystem and even digital banking resources. We wanted to create a way to bring those resources back to our communities. We also agreed that very often, organizations would come into our communities and try to "fix" things without working with the people of the community, which mostly ended up putting the community in more turmoil. Thinking about Daymond John's, FUBU "For Us by Us" slogan. We decided on the slogan "Build with, Not For." This was our own way of saying that you need to build with the people you are serving, not just come in and build for them. Then, in honor of the 4th day of Kwanzaa "Ujamaa," which means Collective Economics, we titled it Ujamaathon. It was the Ujamaa Fintech Hackathon.

I started tapping into my network. Soon I lined up a venue and speakers for the event. I invited Anthony Frasier of the Phat Startup to be our keynote speaker, and he spoke about the history of the black dollar in direct reference to Black Wall Street. Most people had never even heard of it until that day. We had over one hundred attendees, and the event went off almost flawlessly. The sponsor we secured promised us a check of $5K, which would be delivered after the event due to processing times at their company. This was a large, well-recognized company, so we trusted them to follow through.

The event team which now consisted of 4 people myself, the Baruch Alum, Jacob Lee; who was currently the President of Hack for Baruch (one of the first tech and entrepreneurship clubs at Baruch), and John Katt; the NYIT NSBE chapter's Vice President, who would soon be the Illicit Mind technology-focused Board member. We had a decision to make. Could we front the money to source the food and items needed to maintain this 3-day long hackathon? After pulling out my resourcefulness muscle, I carefully looked at possible vendors and created a plan of how we were going to feed and cater to all these humans. We then pooled our funds together and proceeded with the event. We didn't spend the full $5k because we were broke college kids, and didn't have $5k just lying around, but did spend about $1500 collectively. We figured when the sponsor check came and cleared, we would reimburse ourselves and then spend the remaining money on the next Ujamaathon. If we maintained a $1500 budget each time, we could do a series of Ujamaathons with the money. We were planning a whole system of events and activities around this mission of Build with Not for.

The check never came. We never did another Ujamaathon. All our plans for the series and even starting a non-profit to do all this great stuff went down the drain. The Baruch Alum, well he ghosted me, he ghosted us. I don't know if that check ever came in or what happened next. I reached out multiple times to follow up and try to get answers, but those were many failed attempts. Jacob, John, and I stayed connected and continued working together, and we brought some of the Ujamaathon themes and the slogans over to Illicit Mind programming.

I moved the week after the hackathon. I couldn't believe it was already a year since I moved into the studio. Renewing the lease was not an option, Cameron was getting older, and we all needed our space. We had the money to afford a bigger place, so Bryan and I rented a 3-bedroom apartment on the second floor of a three-family house in Newark. Our studio was in East Orange, about a 7-minute drive from where the new apartment was. While in East Orange, we never had any issues related to violence or danger. Although Newark had a bad reputation for being a rough neighborhood, we figured it was a short distance from where we used to be, and we were close to the Bloomfield section of New Jersey which was rumored to be the "good side" of Newark.

After the move, I settled back into planning events, and although they were making a huge impact and building a lot of community, I was burning out and seeing no financial return on investment. That's when I started to actively seek out more work like odd jobs, freelancing, and gigs to make ends meet. As I do when in a bind, I tapped into my network. I reached out to folks I knew, letting them know I was in search of job opportunities.

One of my friends from the Superhero Mastermind group, Gary Riger, responded that his company BKLYN, a software and web development company was indeed looking for someone to help on the design and marketing side. This sounded perfect and convenient as the office was not too far from my school. There was one additional criteria that I actually didn't meet. I had no experience in WordPress. Up until this point, I mostly avoided WordPress and used platforms like Weebly and Wix to build websites. I figured "I have ⅔", I can just google WordPress stuff and figure it out as I go.

I got the job and started working. Things were going well. I was even able to plan a small networking event/workshop in partnership with BKLYN. Then the time came for me to edit a client's WordPress website. I logged in and had no idea what the heck I was looking at. So, I tried to google and came up at a dead end. That's when I realized I would need to re-tap my network. I reached out to my friend, Malcolm Paul, who was a college classmate that I participated in an on-campus app building competition with a few months back. He was from the Caribbean, and when I told him what I was doing with the Caribbean's In Tech group, he was all for it. He helped to build the official website and became a Co-Organizer for the group. Malcolm was a tech wiz, and so I figured he could definitely help. Indeed, he did help me figure out the issue. I was enjoying my time at BKLYN, but I also started to realize maybe I wasn't the best fit for this gig. I was also actively looking for more work at the time.

I saw an opening for an event associate at a Startup Institute. I knew most of the team from volunteering for them in the past, and they had partnered with me for about three Illicit Mind events so far as the venue sponsor. I took a chance and applied. I was hired on as the Summer 2016 events associate. I was paid a monthly stipend, and this was a huge help with my financial situation and huge for Illicit Mind because I had access to the office and the WeWork location we were at, a plus to host events. I also now had access to even more potential speakers through their network.

Startup Institute would be every day with set hours, so I had to leave BKLYN. Gary was amazing and understood. In my mind, I was already thinking of someone that would be a great fit to be on the BKLYN team. Yup, Malcolm. In the few weeks, as I prepared to leave, I formally connected Gary and Malcolm, and in no time, Malcolm became a part of the BKLYN team. Gary had been personally looking for someone with Malcolm's skill set for a while, and after recently quitting his job to set out on his own full-time entrepreneurial venture, they were a perfect fit for each other. Network = Net Worth!

That summer I had a great time at Startup Institute. I was able to sit in on most of the classes, and if I didn't have work to do, I was paying attention to the lessons and taking notes as the students. Everything was going so well that I was extended an offer to stay on board for the Fall Cohort as well. I would get a slight upgrade in my role to being the official NY Events manager.

Illicit Mind was doing well, generating more income than ever before. Throughout the summer at Startup Institute, my coworkers would often refer to me as "Georgie is Getting Shit Done". From hearing that almost every day, an idea started to form in my mind. "What if I held a massive event, my first conference, and call it the Get Shit Done Summit?" I went home and started to plot out how it would work, what the purpose would be, and all the micro details. I wasn't sure how I would pull it off, but I did know for sure that I was going to try.

With all the amazing moments, a bad turn started to rear its ugly head.

One Friday morning I woke up and wasn't feeling well, feeling quite terrible actually. I just assumed it would let up by the end of the day. When it didn't, and I kept having to go to the bathroom, my boss at the Startup Institute suggested that I go to the ER. Bryan picked me up, took me to the ER, and they admitted me. A few hours later, I was in the ICU under anesthetics undergoing an endoscopy. An endoscopy is when they put a long tube down your throat, and it goes into your stomach. Overall, it wasn't that bad because I was put to sleep. That's at least what I thought until I woke up during the last few seconds of the procedure while they were pulling out the tube. I was scared and started to choke.

Turns out that I had a stomach ulcer that erupted and was causing internal bleeding. This literally came out of nowhere. The doctors mentioned that they see this pretty often in immigrants, specifically from the Caribbean; something to do with the region and the types of viruses they have there. All I know it was weird and I was totally thrown off guard.

On Sunday, I was released from the hospital and cleared to go back to work the following week.

A week later, Bryan woke up and went to get the truck to go to work. He called me stating the truck was not where he parked it. I immediately panicked because the night before when I came home around 9 pm from a work event, I saw the truck parked on the corner. We searched a few close streets, and the truck wasn't there. It was gone! We called the cops, but there wasn't much that they could do. We had to cancel the next few days of jobs for Mckoy Movers, and we had to find and buy a new truck. FAST!

This was when another medical emergency popped up at my door. This time it wouldn't be fixed in a weekend, but instead, last around 9 months.

Yup, I was pregnant. I was grateful to be blessed with a pregnancy and a future child, but I was also nervous about what this would mean for my college career, for the job opportunities that I was currently being faced with, for Illicit Mind. Added to this, the stress that came from the truck being stolen and me recently being in the hospital. This was a lot for us to handle. We had much to think about and a lot of decisions to make. Decisions that needed to be made soon because pregnancy brain, hormones, and fatigue were about to kick in, and we needed a plan!

At the center of that plan was getting help! I needed help with Illicit Mind and not just some volunteers, but a committed team. That's when I put out some asks to my network in my quest to find some team members.

John Katt was currently volunteering his time as an Illicit Mind technology board member. When I shared with him, I was looking for a full-time CTO, he was open to taking on that opportunity. John was the first official C-Suite hire.

Then my classmate and friend, Kelly Garcia, forwarded the CFO job description to her boyfriend, Pedro Crespo, who was working in finance at the time, he expressed interest. We did some interviews, and Pedro became a part of our team as well. Now I had a CTO and CFO. I knew I would need a full board as well. I reached out to four mentors I had at the time, Jan Baker, Tanya Alvarez, Ron Summers, and John Lynn, and asked them to be on my advisory board. They all agreed.

Within weeks, this solo operation now had seven people building and working behind Illicit Mind, just by tapping into my network.

We started marketing and planning for the Get Shit Done summit. I tapped my network looking for speakers, a venue, and sponsors. Within a few days, we got over eighty applications for speakers. After an employee from the NY based SaaS company, DigitalOcean, came in to teach a class at Startup Institute, I remembered that back in March I met one of the founders and he said to reach out. DigitalOcean could possibly partner with me for an event, I thought to myself. I reached out, and he said yes! The Get Shit Done summit would be held at Digital Ocean. I got a few more event partners like The Benchmark Creative group, recruited some volunteers, got a few sponsors to donate goodie bags and swag. The summit went from being an idea a few weeks before to a reality taking place in November.

That same summer, I was able to participate in a Leadership program called Startingbloc, all thanks to another tap into my network. Startingbloc is a 5-day intensive program to help changemakers gain leadership skills and clarity in their work and life. The tuition was over $1K, and I knew I didn't have that. By tapping into my network, I was able to fundraise my entire program tuition and then attend the program in August.

Tapping into my network once again had its benefits. This time I increased my net worth. It landed me jobs, got me access, and accelerated the growth of my companies and projects. My network wasn't built off of simple "what can you do for me or I do for you", but off of genuine connections, learning from and building with people. I didn't walk into spaces pretending to be someone I wasn't. I was honest, transparent, took chances, and focused on just being myself. That's how I grew my network.

Do's and Don'ts to Organically Build Your Network

In-person networking

This is when your primary communications with the people are in-person/ face to face. Some platforms that promote in-person networking opportunities include Meetup.com, Eventbrite.com, local city events, Workshops offered by the government, and happy hours.

Do:

- Have meaningful conversations. It's better to talk to 3 people in 2 hours and have valuable conversations that they will remember you for vs. 100 people who won't even remember your name.

- Focus on "How can I add value to this person? What can I offer them?"

- Ask questions. Be a conversation starter.

- Be transparent with who you are and what you do.

Don't

- Run around the room trying to give your business card to everyone while having 30-second conversations (unless its speed networking)

- Focus on "What can I get from this person?"

- Shy away from participating

Online Networking

Where your primary communications with people are done online. Some platforms for this include Facebook, LinkedIn, Slack, Instagram, Twitter, YouTube, and Webinars.

Do

- Ask questions. Be a conversation starter.

- Offer to help others.

- Participate

- Turn on your webcam! Even though it's digital, it's nice to see human faces.

- Be transparent with what you do and how they can refer you.

Don't

- Only try to sell your products/services or just get followers and views.

- Shy away from participating.

- Join too many networks

- Get overly distracted.

The Follow-Up

After you meet someone and get their contact information, send them a message within 24 hours so they can remember you. Ask for another follow-up conversation. Offer some insight or assistance with something they are working on. The key is to CREATE VALUE! GIVE GIVE GIVE

Relationship Building

Networking is the first step in relationship building. You will build that relationship by:

- Communicating

- Showing your value

- Being honest

- Being transparent

- Giving value

Then when the chance comes for that person to refer you to someone who needs your services, there is no hesitation or doubt because they know that you are the perfect person to receive that referral.

What's your Network and Net Worth?

CHAPTER 12

BE HUMBLE

———— ∿∿ ————

> *"God, grant me the serenity to accept the things I*
> *cannot change, the courage to change the things I*
> *can, and the wisdom to know the difference."*
>
> *- James Altucher, The Power of No*

For years now, my social media handle has been "Georgie Be Humble". I don't remember why I chose this or when, but I knew it resonated with me for a long time and became a major part of my life. Being humble grounds me. I am modest with my accomplishments and success. I don't let pride get in the way and think I am too smart, too good, or better than anyone or anything. I don't treat people special because they have more or less than me. I walk around with my heart on my sleeve and my mind open and hungry for interaction and education.

Occasionally, being this humble has had an adverse effect on my life. It makes me naive to certain people and situations, and during my pregnancy, I was very naive about the expectations that I set up. Even with asking for help, I was in way over my head.

I went into this pregnancy with a full-time job, taking full-time classes, a startup, a husband, a 4-year old, and as the president of the Tech club on campus. Back in Spring 2016, I was voted president of the club, Hack for Baruch, which was a club that focused on Tech and Entrepreneurship.

I burned out and fast AF, especially since I was pregnant. I fell asleep practically everywhere. Everything got me upset. I was always tired or distracted. I ended up having to part ways with Startup Institute, I almost failed my classes. Thank God for extra credits. I had a chance to make it all up and had to make the Get Shit Done summit the last event for Illicit Mind 2016. Although at the time I hated online classes, with a baby due in the middle of the semester, I had no choice but to take all my classes online.

With the help of the team, we shifted the mission and vision of Illicit Mind, tightened up our programming, brought on others to help in various capacities, and created a business development strategy that would scale the company. A few events were scheduled around my pregnancy, and I went back to the City as much as possible to convene with the team. We were at this time working out of a WeWork location, as part of an initiative by WeWork that supported diverse and minority founders that Pedro signed us up for. It felt great to have space, and it felt great to watch Illicit Mind growing up and learning to scale like this.

My first pregnancy, I was in high school and didn't have nearly half the responsibilities and obligations I had now. In my mind, I thought this pregnancy and post-baby journey would be easier because I wasn't a single mom, I had jobs and so many other opportunities that I didn't have before. I was totally wrong!

I spent so much time comparing my pregnancies to each other and listening to people's comments about "the second time around being easier", that I took that information as fact. In reality, every pregnancy and every child will be different, respond differently, have a different toll on your life.

March 2017 rolled around, and our lease was ending, so we moved... again. Staying in Newark didn't seem like the best idea especially after incidents like my husband's truck getting stolen off our street, and multiple police raids happening at the house across from us, we came to realize it a trap house.

After weeks of house hunting, we moved about 100 miles away to a town called Port Jervis. The town sat on the cornerstone of NY, NJ, and PA. To me, it felt like the middle of nowhere. There was a very small town vibe, and the rental was a duplex, two connected houses, but for the first time, we didn't have neighbors living above or under us and we had a backyard for the kids to play. I knew it was best for our growing family to be in a safer neighborhood. It wasn't until weeks later, we realized that the "safer neighborhood" came with a dirty little secret. The people were very racist. There were a few black people here and there, but none on our street. When I did see any, it was mostly black men in interracial relationships with white women.

After recently watching Jordan Peele's "Get Out", plus being a Black Studies Minor in college, a racist town in the middle of nowhere, had me shook. I was subconsciously always in a state of panic. Incidents like the first time I saw the Confederate flag, just sitting there all regular on someone's car, or the time I was waiting at the bus stop with some other moms to get our kids off the bus and these moms were referring to each other as "my n*gga".

I was not here for this craziness and counted down the days to when the lease was up so we could LEAVE!

Bryanna was born in April, and then reality came knocking at my door. She was so different from Cameron. I was scared. I was nervous and questioned if I was doing this right because I couldn't even remember clearly most of Cameron's early days. My grandma and Mrs. Jenkins were by my side almost every day for the first two months with Cameron. We lived so far this time around, that family and friends could only come by for a few days or even hours at a time. Bryan had work and Cameron was being homeschooled until the Fall. He was five years old and relatively independent, but he was still a baby and needed my support and direction, and Bryanna was a newborn and needed it too.

I was still trying to keep up with my online classes and run Illicit Mind from a distance, all in the same breath. There was too much on my plate, and I still had this idea that I was superwoman and could handle it all.

The worst part is I kept adding things to my plate to stay busy to "feel like myself" to be the "Get Shit Done Georgie". As part of our 'new baby plan', I would stay home with the baby for a year. I agreed to this. But in my head, I felt this meant I would become a kept woman, a stay-at-home mom.

At the time, my view of a stay-at-home mom was someone who had it easy, didn't have to work, and mostly depended on the man to bring home the bacon. This ideology was torn to shambles in my first few weeks of staying home. I was working 10 times harder than before. The minute I opened my eyes, I was on the clock until the minute my eyes closed to go to bed. With a newborn, off clock didn't exist. We had to wake up every 2 -3 hours to eat or play.

The meal preparation, handling laundry, maintaining a clean home, doing work sessions with Cameron, and then my work responsibilities, and my online classes, whoo! It was a lot!

June 2017 came around; it was time for a day that I had been working towards for the last 22 years of my life. It was time to graduate from college. I was able to complete my final few classes with decent enough grades. This time around, I had two babies in the crowd, my husband, and a list of strong women in my life including my grandma Lorraine, Mrs. Jenkins, my godmother, Julie, and my two aunts, Andria and Vinola.

Blog via LinkedIn Pulse

Title: 5 Years. 4 Jobs. 3 Startups. 2 Kids. 1 Husband & 0 Debt later...

Originally Published: June 8th, 2017

This past Monday, June 5th, 2017, I became a graduate of Baruch College. After 5 long years, working for 4 different companies, being a part of 3 startups, having two kids, and getting married, my college career is now over.

There were many times along this journey that I wanted to quit school. I felt mostly that school was getting in my way and not allowing me to focus and excel at the things I wanted to do. Now that school is over, I don't regret it one bit. I am actually happy I stayed and that I no longer have to spend most of my days and nights doing class/homework though. Now it's time to put on my work boots and go full steam ahead.

What Next?

Taking some time off! I have been enrolled in school since I was two years old. That means for the last twenty years I've been going to school. While various parts of my life changed, transformed, and grew, school remains a constant. I'm taking the next year to work remotely while enjoying all the ever-changing things that have happened in my life.

Get Shit Done. While working remotely, I will continue to develop my startups, personal brand, and offer services part-time, that way by this time next year I can dive head-first into the workforce and hit the ground running!

Continue learning. I've always self-taught myself, and I'm a firm believer that to achieve greatness you must never stop learning. I am ready to take my lifelong education into my own hands.

Sharing. I plan to start actively writing and posting on my blog again (in the past year, I fell off a bit). These past years in college, I've learned and experienced so much. There were good, bad, ugly and hilarious moments that don't deserve to be kept to myself. I want to share my journey with others to inspire, teach, and engage. Stay tuned!

Follow my journey through my website
www.georgieann.com

Full force adulting in...5...4...3...2...1 #Classof2017 WE DID IT!

Now with school off my long lists of tasks and creating a few systems to help me maintain my hectic lifestyle, I was getting into my own head again. Most of my classmates were starting jobs in the Fall, and I felt as though I didn't have enough to keep me busy. I was on a one-way track to burn out.

I should've taken this time to rest, to plan, to work on myself, and to rejuvenate, but I did exactly the opposite, then in August 2017, I committed myself to even more unneeded work.

Blog from GeorgieBeHumble (Medium)

Title: When Life Gives You Work from Home, You Create a YouTube channel.

Originally published: August 17th, 2017

Over the next year or so I will be working remotely from home. As the extremely social person I am, this started to drive me nuts! I've worked remotely for the last 2/3 years, but I participated in many meetup groups, hosted events, and co-worked a bunch. Now having to stay home the majority of the week was slowly driving me to insanity. I wanted to see people, to interact with people, and connect with people. Hence, I decided to start a YouTube and Facebook Live series!

Here is how I did it.

First, a name. I needed something interesting, catchy, and something that represented me. Aha! I chose the name Get Shit Done with Georgie. This was a semi-pun on my surname "Getton", because all my life people have said thing like "Georgie-Ann Getting it done" or "Georgie Getting shit done." It was a perfect name.

Next, I had to figure out how I would execute this because I'm the queen of Getting Shit Done. I took to the internet to learn how to record, direct, publish, and stream videos. After hours of doing research and testing tools, I created a special formula that uses OBS Software, YouTube, Zoom, Google Hangouts, YouTube Live, Facebook Live, and Windows movie maker [I will be teaching a course on this formula in September stay tuned].

Then, I had to figure out what I would be presenting on my channel. What is my why? The purpose of Get Shit Done with Georgie. After writing down all the things I could talk about and do on my channel, I then consulted a few folks. I decided on teaching tech-based tools, sharing my tech ecosystem experiences, and featuring some of the coolest, most awesome people I know to do a live Q&A.

On to agenda. How often would I be posting? When should people be expecting content? I selected Tuesday and Wednesday for releasing tech-based tool tutorials and sharing my experiences. Then Thursdays for the live series. [Subscribe to my YouTube and Facebook to always know when videos are up!]

I had my name, my tools, my purpose, and my agenda. What else did I need? Well, maybe a way to make money from doing these videos, because regardless of how passionate I am, I do need electricity and Wi-Fi to produce this content, and you know food to stay alive [ahh, the simple things in life].

This led me to create a Patreon! What's a Patreon? Well go to Patreon.com/gsdwithgeorgie and watch my intro video to understand what it is and how it works. [TL; DR Patreon allows individuals… like yourself… to donate a set amount per month to my work as a creator.]

SOO recap.

Name … Check!

Tools… Check!

Purpose… Check!

Agenda…Check!

Income… Sorta Check [Need some patrons to actually sign up]

What's Last?!

This post is the last step. Letting the world know what I'm doing and getting it done. Join me tonight at facebook.com/gsdwithgeorgie for the very first episode of Get

Shit Done with Georgie. I will be featuring Chike Ukaegbu from Startup 52.

Yea, I was pushing myself to the edge and breaks didn't exist. I felt because I already had a self-help journey with books, mentorship, and therapy, that I was good; I could handle this because I knew better. I had built a foundation. But I couldn't handle it, and my foundation was cracking. Don' t worry though, life came in again and snatched the wheel out my hand even faster than it did the first time. I should have taken a break, but instead, I burned out.

Burnouts vs. Breaks

For a long time, I confused being burnt out for taking a break. How did this happen?

The simple answer is having a lack of boundaries, an unclear understanding of my limits and flat out lying to myself. I would work myself so hard, literally day in and day out to complete my tasks, and then I literally couldn't go anymore. I would say to myself "okay now I'll take a break," but it wasn't really a break because I literally couldn't continue even if I tried. It wasn't until recently when I came to the realization that if I stayed on this path, I would not only be less productive, but I would ruin my health along the way. Here is how I solved this very unhealthy problem (and you can too).

Step 1: Differentiation

You need to identify and differentiate what is healthy and what is unhealthy

Recognizing burnout (The things that are unhealthy)

- You don't want to do anything
- You find yourself doing very unproductive things that cost energy (randomly scrolling through emails and social media but not interacting)
- You don't eat or sleep properly
- You start tasks but can't focus then shift to doing very unimportant tasks

Taking Breaks (The things that are Healthy)

- Purposely setting aside times to relax
- Still having the energy to direct in your break activity
- Sleeping and eating on time and properly
- Doing things on purpose

Step 2: Boundaries

I used to take on tasks and roles that I was good at even though I wasn't necessarily passionate about doing them. I thought it would help build my skill set and resume. But as time went on, I realized that not because I'm good or even great at something means I should do that thing. Passion is one of my biggest drivers, and when I do things that I'm not passionate about, I can't fully show up. I decided to create a list of 4 topics (industries) that I was passionate about AND I was good at. Then I went on to create a list of 4 emotions I wanted to feel about any new role/task I was offered. Creating these allowed me to limit the things I said yes to and only participate in things that I could show up and be fully 100% present in.

Step 3: Honesty

Be honest with yourself and those around you. If you're tired, say so. If a project is due in two days, but you know you need 3 days to complete it, say so. You must be honest because if you burn yourself out or push too far beyond your limits, you will end up producing half-assed work or worse, not completing the work at all.

These three steps have helped me to separate Burnout from Breaks. It's important to take care of yourself. Take breaks, relax, hang out with friends and family. Visit social media to socialize sometimes, and not to just market or do research. As we all know "you can't pour from an empty cup".

Now ask yourself:

- When was your last break?
- When is your next break?

Other ways to set boundaries

Set specific times to reply to emails. Ex: No emails from Friday night to Sunday Morning

Set times to watch TV or do something fun

Have a 'Me' day. Ex: One or two days out of the month, take a day for yourself. No phone, no computer, no work, just kickback. It may be hard at first, but trust me, 24 hours isn't going to set you back as much as you think.

Use the Do Not Disturb phone/laptop feature. Ex: I set my phone on do not disturb every night from 10 pm-6 am. I had a bad habit of thinking that every notification I received needed my immediate attention (it actually doesn't). On "do not disturb" I don't hear or see the notifications. It helps.

Blog post via @Georgiebehumble on Medium

Title: The Art of Getting Shit Done

Originally Published: September 17th, 2017

This will one day be the title of my New York Times Bestselling book. When is that exactly, I'm not sure, possibly 2019, but for today, it is the title of my blog post that will go viral[the universe is always listening, affirm what you want and you will get it].

My life has always been about getting shit done. From walking before the age of 1 yr. old to being a mother of 2, college graduate, and wife at the age of 22 [p.s I'm currently 22].

People are constantly amazed at the things I do and are shocked at the fact that I can even do them in the first place. A colleague once told me that by the age of 26, I'll be Beyoncé on a unicorn. That makes me tear up a bit. How can someone see so much magic in me?

Truth be told, I don't have any secret 12 step formulas or 4-hour productivity routines. I have a specific mindset. I wake up and say, "Today I am going to get shit done." I've learned that getting shit done isn't a science with some magic formula, it is an art. You have three primary colors [limited resources], and you are then tasked with creating the rainbow of your life.

As I begin to develop my personal brand and expand my business, I want to help others build a mindset similar to mine where they can see the rainbow of potential in their palette of 3 primary colors. It's never about what you have, it's about what you do with it.

Now about the book. I have been thinking about it for a year now, and I finally began to write it in July. Below is what I have so far:

Note from the Author.

Hey Reader,

This note is going to be quick and to the point. Here I am at 1:21 am on Saturday, July 15th, 2017 FINALLY writing this guide. I started it November 5th, 2016, after I held the very first Get Shit Done summit in NYC. I would write bits in a notebook, other bits in my phone, more bits on post-it notes. Just a shit ton of bits everywhere. No more bits! I have decided it's time to get in front of the computer and Get This shit done.

First, who the heck am I? My name is Georgie-Ann Getton-Mckoy. Yes, it's a mouthful, so most people call me Georgie, and I'm totally fine with that. I am currently 22 years old, Baruch College graduate with a B.S in Graphic Communications as of June 2017, mother to Cameron and Bryanna and wife to Bryan, Founder of Illicit Mind Inc, Entrepreneur, Diversity in Tech Enthusiast, speaker, and last but not least, the Queen of Getting shit done.

Second, why should you read this book? If you want to develop a doer mindset, this is the book you read. I've had to step out of my comfort zone, push my limits, become super resourceful, and literally reprogram my whole mindset to get where I am today. I want to share that information with you so that you can too. You should read this book if you're going to stop wasting time and start Getting Shit Done.

Third, what to expect. Expect the unexpected! That's what you should expect. Expect a bunch of grammatical errors, whatever Grammarly free version doesn't pick up, will stay. Expect a bunch of shits, fucks, damns, and more. I mean you decided to read a book called The Art of Getting Shit Done, so I assume "sentence enhancers" won't offend you. Expect me to be raw and real. I will NOT be sugar coating anything. If you don't like the truth, well wrong book, sis.

Fourth, we've already wasted enough time. Let's Get this shit done already!

Ohh, I know that totally got you pumped. The book will include many stories of my life and how I have used the Art of Getting Shit Done mentally to constantly create rainbows.

[Quick Insider] Stories include:

- How I finished high school on time while giving birth in the middle of senior year

- How I graduated college while again giving birth in the middle of senior year

- How I got into a startup Accelerator in my Junior year of college

- Why I got kicked out the first time as a teen

- What I did when I got kicked out the second time as a young mom.

- How I created a 100+ person summit with less than $1k

- How my food for my first ever event was bought with a food stamps card

- How I quit my full-time job at 19 while being a single mom

- How I got an entirely free ride to college

And that's just the beginning. While I work on the book, I will periodically release insiders from it. Until then, follow me on Medium and Facebook to see how I Get Shit Done.

The Get Shit Done summit was coming up again. I got excited, and that made me excited to go back and complete this book as well. November 2017 rolled around, and we did the 2nd GSD summit. This time I knew what to expect, and it was fancier and more organized than the first year. Everyone was saying how proud they were of Illicit Mind and me, and they couldn't wait for more.

What they didn't know was that everything was about to change. After the GSD summit, I went into a state of depression.

I didn't want to do anything.

I was starting to feel the same way I did back in 2014. As though the world saw me as this perfect well put together, hard working person, but on the back end, I was barely holding the thing together. This time around, I was upset with myself because I had experienced this before, I should have known better.

CHAPTER 13

LEVEL UP

> *"If you do not change you can become extinct."*
>
> *- Spencer Johnson*

It was now December 2017 and my birthday was close. I started to do my annual reflection on my life. It was clear that I needed to make some tough decisions and I couldn't do it alone. I reached out to various friends and family members that I trusted to help get some clarity and insights. My friend and colleague, Tani Chambers, suggested that I do three things:

- Complete her "Life Plan" workbook that she created for the entrepreneurs she coached.

- I read the book "The One Thing" by Gary Keller.

- I created a vision board of what I wanted my "Life to look like."

I did all three steps. This gave me enough clarity and foundation to create the next steps. It was as though a window opened up for me while in a dark room and this brief moment of light shined upon my face.

From doing the Life Plan, I realized that I needed to prioritize the things I gave my time and attention to. One of the activities was to create a vision statement around each of my top 5 priorities.

- Family - to mature as a unit while growing and loving each other unconditionally

- Personal Development - to be confident and grounded in my truth

- Spiritual Life - to have faith and guidance that there is more, and I am worthy of it

- Health - to feel refreshed and alive every moment of my existence

- Career - to pursue wealth building and positive impact around the world

From doing the vision board, I was able to see what I wanted to accomplish in the next year, and as a very visual person, this helped me to start thinking of ways to get these things done.

From reading "The One Thing", I learned the habit of doing one thing at a time, and it made me realize that multitasking is a lie. When I looked back on the times in my life when I did my best, it was when I had multiple tasks to complete but did them one at a time.

Each day, I was improving myself 1% and getting to a better place mentally. I made a conscious effort to do more things that I loved, but slowly so that I wouldn't burn out. This shift in myself allowed my family to grow, Illicit Mind to expand, more job opportunities and doors to open up for me. I started reading and attending events again.

March was here, and our lease was coming to an end again, and this time another big change was about to happen. Bryan had enlisted in the Navy and was set to leave in July. After multiple discussions, we figured it best that the kids and I stay with my family in Long Island while he did boot camp. After that ended, we would make decisions about the next steps depending on where he was based.

His parents had gotten engaged and they were getting married in Jamaica in May.

Our plan was to extend our lease one month till April, then move to Long Island in May, go to Jamaica, then once we came back, the countdown to boot camp would begin.

This was the first time I was going back to Jamaica without my family. I was nervous but excited to go back "home". What I wasn't prepared for was the huge culture shock that I would get while in Jamaica.

Upon my return from Jamaica, I wrote a self-reflective essay on my experience, but I didn't share it until August.

Post via GSD with Georgie Blog

Title: I will always work harder than you

Originally posted: 8/10/2018

My kids and their cousins. The FUTURE!

I will ALWAYS work harder than you.

This past May I spent two weeks in Jamaica. The majority of my time was spent in the parish of St. Thomas where my husband and I grew up. I left when I was 7 yrs. old, and he left at 18 yrs. old. This community is also one of the poorest and most underdeveloped parishes on the island.

As I was taking in the fresh island air, views, and just overall good vibes, I couldn't help but think, "I truly need to be grateful for the access and opportunities I have living in America." I also thought about how privileged I was to have grown up in the United States, and in New York to be specific.

If you aren't familiar with the way the immigration and visa system work, let me break it down for you. Most often, people only get visas for working or going to school. You spend hundreds, even thousands of dollars applying for those visas, and there is no guarantee that you will get one.

Let's say you're one of the lucky ones to be granted a visa. You then get to travel to the US, with a limited amount of time that you are allowed to stay in the country. Time can range from one month to a few years (based on the visa purpose). Most people try to get school visas then land a job before the visa expires so that the job can then sponsor them. (When a job application asks, "Will you need a visa sponsorship?", that's the reason why that question is there).

Well, that was a brief overview (I summed it all up fairly quickly, but immigration is often a long and tedious process). Anyway, back to my family. My uncle was able to get a visa. He then came to the US and got a green card which meant he became a permanent resident. After 10 years of permanent residency, you're able to apply to become a US citizen. He applied and got through. At that point, he was then able to "File" (put in an application with immigration so that another member of your family can migrate to the US) for his parents, my grandmother, and grandfather. After spending time and money again, they were approved and came to the US where they then also did their 10 years to become citizens. After these 10 years, my grandparents then filed for their children which included my mother, two uncles, and my aunt. You may be thinking "why didn't your uncle file for his siblings?" Great question! Another fun feature of immigration is that you can only file for certain relatives such as parents, kids, and spouses. My mother was able to bring my two brothers and me with her because we were considered dependent children, and grandparents can file for underage grandchildren. So myself, two brothers, and two cousins were also able to make the trip to the US.

For me to be here right now sitting in the US as a citizen, it started with my uncle getting approved for that original visa. Let's remember that not all families are this lucky or have yet put in the amount of time it took to get their families to the US.

This is why I will always work harder than you. On my back, I hold the future generations of my family. Before I was even born, actions were being made to ensure I didn't grow up without access and opportunities. Steps were being taken even before my uncle was born, before my grandparents were born. Everything that happened from the first slave ship with my ancestors who were taken from Africa and brought to Jamaica to grow sugar cane, has led me to where I am today. I am literally my ancestors' wildest dreams.

In Black Panther, Erik Killmonger said the unforgettable line "bury me in the ocean like my ancestor who jumped off the ships because they refused to be enslaved." My ancestors didn't jump, because they had a dream. That dream was that one day their successors would be smashing ceilings and changing the world.

So, for me to be right here right now, I must thank those who came before and set an example for my children and my successors.

My children are first-generation Jamaican-American, with access and opportunities more than triple what I was born with, and I have to make sure that my great, great-grandchildren have even more than that. A task that will take continuous hard work and dedication similar to what my ancestors have put in, but oh so necessary.

In June right after we came back from Jamaica, I had a few Illicit Mind events planned, started working for CSE Incubator, which had now become CUNY Startups, and had applied to Entrepreneurship Essentials and online program offered by HBX | Harvard Business School.

I was so happy to be back in my element around a community that was warm and welcoming.

That's when the bad news came. Because of some paperwork issues, Bryan was no longer leaving for the NAVY in July. We had to now make some tough decisions, and fast. Do we stay in Long Island until whenever things get sorted out? Do we rent another apartment? Or do we move out of state like we had spoken about in the past?

At the same time, I was going through a huge internal shift. Being back in NY and doing events and being in the startup ecosystem again, I didn't have the same feeling that I did before. It felt more of a drag, a "do I have to do it?" instead of I want to do this.

Overall, I had to decide. What comes next, for everything!

My company, my family, my life, my wellness. In the end, it came down to one answer.

I needed to reset. A fresh, clean slate to start over.

That's what we did. Bryan and I took a road trip to Georgia in the middle of August. We looked at some homes, selected one, put in our application.

By September 1st, we now lived 1000 miles away from our friends and family in NY, Illicit Mind was shut down, and there was nothing on my plate.

I reset and had space and clarity for the first time in a long time to decide what comes next. How can I level up!?

Post via GSD with Georgie Blog

Title: It's not goodbye, it's just see you later

Originally Published: 9/5/2018

In 2015, I (Georgie) took a leap of faith with the goal of creating a community of innovators, creatives and entrepreneurs ready to learn and grow together. I launched Illicit Mind because as a diverse young entrepreneur I lacked the tools, network and support systems that were necessary to be a successful entrepreneur. After 3 years, what started as a 1-woman operation, with much blood, sweat, tears and hard work, has turned into something so much more.

We are incredibly proud to say we have had the pleasure of working with some AMAZING team members, held over 60 events, engaged over 3000 innovators, and have opened many doors for ourselves and our peers.

The road has not been smooth, but it has been worth it. Along the way, we have come across many problems that innovators face on a day to day basis. Ranging from access to financial and social capital, lack of diversity in tech, lack of community support, too many resources, and not sure how to execute their idea. We have tapped into solving each of these problems through our programming in various ways.

With time, things change. Illicit Mind has come to a point where for the team and work to grow and continue, the company itself must come to an end. It saddens us to announce that we have decided to shut down Illicit Mind. The team will continue to work in the innovation and impact space with a focus on helping diverse innovators succeed. This is not a goodbye, but a see you later.

A special note from John:

John, the CTO of Illicit Mind, is continuing his work of building with diverse entrepreneurs, products that put impact at the forefront of their mission. One part of this will be the continuation of the "Build With, Not For" podcast, where John along with Pedro Crespo will delve into topics facing the diverse entrepreneur today. Topics will range from technology, business, product development, user acquisition, and many more of the challenges faced by entrepreneurs. John and Pedro will discuss concepts taken from leading minds in entrepreneurship and explore how they can be implemented by the doer and hustler. The occasional guest will also join the podcast to give insights into their entrepreneurship journey, providing valuable knowledge from the trenches!

John will also be aiding and consulting teams looking to take their idea to the next level. If a team needs that extra set of eyes to help them get to the next level or merely needs advice on a specific topic related to tech or product development, John will be available for free consultations. If teams need more of a consistent presence to consult and guide them over a period of time, John also will be offering consulting services. To get in touch with John you can reach him by email: john@piao.nyc or socials: Twitter @JRK18 LinkedIn:

https://www.linkedin.com/in/johnkatt/

A special note from Pedro:

Pedro Crespo, our CFO, will be returning to the world of real estate at the brokerage firm, Triplemint. He will be helping individuals and families find their place in the beautiful metropolis of New York City. There he will assist with the full spectrum of RE activities such as Luxury Rentals, Buy, and Sales. Pedro, along with John Katt, will also be continuing Build With Not For podcast where they will be talking about the entrepreneurial journey that the trials and errors that most entrepreneurs face in their attempt to be their own bosses or change agents. He can be reached at <ins>pedro@triplemint.com</ins> Twitter: @PedroICrespo

https://www.linkedin.com/in/pcrespo1/

A special note from Georgie:

Georgie, the CEO and Founder of Illicit Mind plans to relaunch her GSD with Georgie brand. This will include a YouTube channel, webinars, digital content, classes, and coaching services. She has gained so much knowledge, connections and resources in the past years as an entrepreneur, mom, wife, student, and creative. It's now time to share how she hacked both her personal and professional life to achieve work-life synergy. Contact me at Georgie@gsdwithgeorgie.com (My georgie@illicitmind.com still forwards to me also). Or on social

@gsdwithgeorgie (same for IG, Twitter) or Linkedin.com/in/gsdwithgeorgie

Before I go, there are some people I'd like to say some thank you's to:

First, I thank God for giving me the strength to persevere and grow this company. Thank you to my family and friends for supporting me through this journey; Bryan, Cameron, Bryanna, Sharna, Julie, Andria, Lorraine, Christoff, Collin, Taniko, Marlene, Christina, Jadzia, and Shaina. Whether it was babysitting so I could do an event, or giving me a ride, or coming to an event to assist me, I really appreciate it.

Thank you, John, Pedro, Marvin, Sidni, Tachand, Malcolm, Ofure, Kevin, Cassandra, Shellie, and Iain for the time you spent on our team.

Thank you, Tanya Alvarez, Jan Baker, John Lynn, and Ron Summers for being a great board of advisers. Thank you, Mita, Tani, Faith, TeLisa, Daniel, Kerry-Ann, Tiffany, and Tasha for your various support.

Thank you to all the coworking and offices that have housed our events such as WeWork, Startup Institute, Rise NYC, Digital Ocean, Impact Hub NYC, General Assembly, and many more.

Thank you to everyone who has ever attended an event, been a speaker, a judge, a mentor, an advocate, and friend to Illicit Mind. If I didn't list your name directly, I'm sorry but thank you!!

Thank you all for being a part of this crazy journey with me. The Illicit Mind book has closed, but there is much, much more ahead. Stay tuned 💔🍂▦

Post via GSD with Georgie Blog

Title: Apples to Peaches: Why I moved to Georgia

Originally Posted: 9/6/2018

After living in NY for the last 16* years (2 yrs. in NJ), this August, my family and I took a massive leap of faith.

We moved 1000 miles from NY: Apple to GA: Peach.

From jam-packed high-paced city life to open space, slow motion country life. From friends and family around the corner to strangers and a whole new city and state.

Why the heck would we do such a thing? The simple answer is for peace of mind.

The more complicated answer is a build-up of the last 3 years living in various NY and NJ neighborhoods. In May 2015, we moved to East Orange, NJ. A year later in April 2016, we moved to Newark, NJ. A year later, this time in March 2017, we moved to Port Jervis, NY.

Each year we moved for two main reasons: the community was either not suitable for kids and families, or the apartment had become way too small for our family.

So, back to the simple answer. We wanted a place to call home that could offer us an excellent family-friendly community and enough physical (and mental) space. After all, your home is supposed to be a sanctuary... right?

Moving 1000 miles away has met those needs. Sometimes, you need a change in your environment, to realign yourself, your life and for my family. This move was it. Being a New Yorker for most of my life, I keep trying to convince myself of ways we could have made NY living work, but with a 1- bedroom apartment easily going for over $1,500 and being the size of a closet, it just didn't make sense. I remind myself (daily), "NY is only a plane/train/bus/car ride away."

It's been a week in our new home, and we all LOVE it! The community is amazing, very friendly, kind/neighborly, and diverse. Inside the house is even better. We have more than enough space, including a heavenly master suite and a huge backyard. I have an actual home office now! YAYYY.

We are more productive, happier, eating better, and just taking things one day at a time. The apple was sweet, and peaches are just as sweet.... maybe even sweeter!

Post via GSD with Georgie Blog

Title: What's next for Georgie

Originally Posted: 9/7/2018

Over the last two days, I've made some pretty big announcements. My startup shut down and I moved to Georgia. I received a ton of messages from friends, family, and just general supporters asking me "What's next" and wishing me luck in my future endeavors.

Well, what's next for me? A few things are in the works

I am relaunching my GSD with Georgie brand. This brand houses the Annual GSD summit*, YouTube channel, webinars, digital content, books, classes, and coaching services. I've gained so much knowledge, connections, and resources in the past years as an entrepreneur, mom, wife, student, and creative. It's now time to share how I hacked both my personal and professional life to achieve work-life synergy. Learn more and join the newsletter at gsdwithgeorgie.com. *Yes, the GSD Summit will be happening again for its 3rd year in a row with a small spin for this year. details at getshitdone.xyz*

I am working to grow the CITE Collective as this is an initiative that is very close to my heart, but I haven't put enough of my time and attention into it over the last few years. Check out the work we are doing to support Caribbean's in Tech and Entrepreneurship at CITEcollective.com.

I am freelancing and taking on contracts again. If you need a systems and operations overhaul, growth hacking, web design, graphic design, 1-on-1 coaching, and workshops, here you go! Visit gsdsolutions.xyz to set up a free consultation for us to go over your needs and how I can assist.

That's what I'm doing professionally. Personally, I will be reflecting on the lessons I've learned over the past years and the experiences I've gained. I will also be focusing on my family and home life.

I'm excited for all the things and adventures that are to come, not rushing or overthinking, just grateful and humble.

Thanks in advance for the support.

Post via GSD with Georgie Blog

Title: Year of the Butterfly

Originally Published: 12/21/2018

In Jan 2018, my friend Jadayah and I became accountability partners using the CoJourn Accountability system. CoJourn asks you to set a "theme" and "intention" for your year. My theme was "Year of the butterfly", because my intention was coming out of my cocoon and back into the real world on my terms. To better understand that, I have to take you back to December 2017.

In December 2017, I was in a very dark place. I felt overworked, lonely, unappreciated, and as though I was existing on the terms of others instead of living a life of my own. I had graduated from college, became a 2nd-time mom, and moved over a hundred miles away from most friends and family. I could feel the essence of myself slipping away each day. I didn't want to get out of bed much less leave my room, new projects didn't excite me. I was just not the same "Georgie" anymore.

Silently I was waiting for someone to come and help me find myself again, but deep down, I knew the only person who could help me, who could SAVE me, was… ME.

Slowly I started to get out of bed more, started to search in old journals and blog posts to "find myself". While reading my old journals, I reflected on how much I had changed over the years, and I realized that I've also matured and grown. Unfortunately, this led me to the conclusion that I wouldn't find 2018 Georgie in these books, I would only learn about who I used to be. I could, though, look at the patterns and trends of when I was the BEST Georgie, what circumstances (both good and bad) and environments produced the BEST Georgie's. This new approach helped me to discover a pattern.

When I put myself out into the world on my own terms and just unapologetically asked questions, explored, gave value, took chances, and had fun, I was the BEST Georgie for not only myself, but for the others around me. I started with a vision and then created an execution plan of HOW I would reinvent myself and bring forward the best possible Georgie.

Some key elements to this included:

- Getting my finances in order -> I started consciously saving and financial planning

- Getting my mental health in order - > I got a therapist through Talkspace

- Saying no to things -> "Not because I can, means I should" became my new motto

- Removing things and people who were no longer a good fit in my life -> I unfriended IRL and unfollowed some friends and FAMILY who simply put... just weren't right for me or to me.

- Love Myself out loud and FIRST -> Practicing self-care and what that looked like for me, was reading, working (yes, work makes me happy), learning, dancing, eating more yummy foods.

- Forgiving everyone from my past who has ever hurt me physically, mentally, or emotionally -> I realized I was carrying around a lot of baggage from the past and it seeped into my present day. It was as if the people who have hurt me put a stamp on me stating I was "Damaged Goods". I am my experiences and my journey, it was far from perfect, but this is my story, and I own it. I refuse to give my power to anyone and anything that does not serve me well.

I slowly started to unravel my cocoon. I attended events again, hosted events, did speaking engagements, read and took classes, worked with companies that were creating impact, and just say YES to the things that would pour into Georgie being able to produce and provide her BEST.

Throughout this journey, I feel as though I've finally stepped back into my own shoes. I'm creating and putting myself out there while having fun. My stress level and things I allow to stress me have significantly decreased. I have come out of that dark place and embraced the light. I made some of the HARDEST decisions about life this year, all in the pursuit of being the BEST Georgie.

I can say proudly that I accomplished most of my goals this year and came out of my cocoon as I planned.

Next Year is going to be my "Year of the Lion". I am going to be fierce, shine bright, take charge, and lead. I realized that I don't shine as bright as I know I can due to a fear of outshining others, being judged, being "that girl", but I realize that these are lies I tell myself to stay humble. I can be humble and also celebrate and blaze my trail of greatness at the same time!

Things I got done in 2018

I often silence my wins. The next part of this post is my attempt to share my accomplishments this year with the world.

Books I Read: 24.5 (Haven't finished Becoming...YET!)

- I'm Judging you - Luvvie

- The One Thing - Gary Keller

- You Need More Money - Matt Manero

- Year of Yes - Shonda Rhimes

- Don't dumb down your Greatness - Anthony Frasier

- You're not that great - Elan Gale

- David and Goliath - Malcolm Gladwell

- Awkward Black Girl - Issa Rae

- Black Privilege - Charlemagne Tha God

- Outliers - Malcolm Gladwell

- The four agreements - Don Miguel Ruiz

- What I know for sure - Oprah Winfrey

- The subtle art of not giving a fuck - Mark Manson

- Yes Please - Amy Poehler

- So Close to Being the Sh*t, Y'all Don't Even Know - Retta

- The Defining Decade - Meg Jay, PhD

- Unfu*k Yourself - Gary John Bishop

- Between the World and Me - Ta-Nehisi Coates

- The Life-Changing Magic of Tidying Up - Marie Kondo

- The Last Black Unicorn - Tiffany Haddish

- Linchpin: Are You Indispensable? - Seth Godin

- We're going to Need more wine - Gabrielle Union

- Self-Inflicted Wounds - Aisha Tyler

- The mother of black Hollywood - Jennifer Lewis

- Becoming - Michelle Obama

Classes I've taken: 2

- Udacity - Front End Developer

- HBX | Harvard Business School - Entrepreneurship Essentials

Interviews & Talks: 7

- Carry on Friends Being Caribbean In Tech with Georgie-Ann Getton Mckoy & Malcolm Paul

- Young Boss Media Master Plan Season 2 Episode 4: Georgie-Ann Getton Mckoy of Get Shit Done Summit

- Blacks in Tech Interview "Building A Startup While in College" w/ Georgie-Ann Getton-McKoy

- Secret Birds Caribbean Interview Podcast Episode 68 with Georgie-Ann in the USA via Jamaica. Being a Young, Black, Caribbean Woman in Tech & Entrepreneurship

- Maven.io Conference Digital Storytelling & Disruptive Hacktivism Panel

- East Bronx Academy for the Future Graduation Keynote

Awards: 3

- Echoing Green Future of Work Competition - Top 8

- eBay Startup Cup NY - Top 25
- Ignite Caribbean 30 Under 30 - 2018 30 Under 30 Honoree

What's Next?

- My Goals for 2019
- 15 Speaking Opportunities
- Read 30 books
- Take 3 Classes/Educational Opportunities
- 5 Awards

In the end, there is no perfect formula for how to get shit done. It's simply art. We are all born into this world with a blank canvas. It's our job to create a masterpiece on that canvas. That is The Art of Getting Shit Done.

Every day I am surrounded by people who love and value me, whether they are right here next to me or communicating with me through a piece of technology. Depression still lurks, but it no longer lives here.

Over the last few years, I have developed so much, and each day I grow and learn more. I no longer say things like "therapy is for crazy people", because it's not, and it's a huge stigma that society needs to overcome. I have gained so much more respect for stay-at-home moms because this stuff ain't easy! Self-help/care, mental health, and a constant state of growth literally saved my life.

Go out into the world, level up, make magic! And most importantly …...

GET SHIT DONE!

ACKNOWLEDGMENTS

My little book that I started back in 2016 after boldly hosting a public event called "The Get Shit Done Summit", is now complete and about to make its way into the world in 2019.

I couldn't have written this book without the support and assistance of so many amazing people in my life.

First, I'd like to thank God, who I often refer to as "the universe" for steering me in the right direction, protecting me, and loving me.

Second, I want to thank my family and friends.

My husband, Bryan for being an essential element of support.

My children, Cameron and Bryanna, for showing your momma patience and gratitude.

My tribe, my community of strong women that inspire me daily; my Mom, Grandma Lorraine, Aunty Julie, Aunty Yvonne, Mrs. Jenkins, Grandma Dorcas, Aunty Rob, Jan, Heather, Tanya, Tani, Christina, and Jadzia. My Dad, Carlton, and Uncle Anthony for teaching me persistence and entrepreneurial work ethic.

My siblings Christoff, Collin, and Carltrice for their help on all my business ventures.

My team that helped me write and edit my thoughts, Mellany Paynter and Shannon Simpson.

Third, I want to thank all those who supported my pre-order campaign; Anthony Atkinson & Family, Elisabeth Cardiello & Legacy Out Loud, Chloe Rice, Khadisha Smikle, Lawrence DeRoche', Tanisha and Rolando Hyman, Alexis Siriani, Ana Zorrilla, Andria Robinson, Arthur Lewin, Cara Rose, Christina Bryan, Dale Robinson, Daniel Adeyanju, David Nebinski, Derrick Stroman, Devin Jackson, Edwin Aristor, Einstein Ntim, Emanuel Gathers, Faith Fraser, Gary Riger, Jacob Lee, Jadayah Spencer, Jan Baker, Jazmin Deroche, Jennell Boone, John Katt, Johnson Boateng, Katya Dreyer-Oren, Keianna Dixon, Kelly Wolf, Ken Chester, Lloyd Cambridge, Maria-Leena Kerr, Michael Mckoy, Mikhail Martin, Molly Keehn, Olive Persimmon, Pedro Crespo, Rodney Agnant, Sabrina Golding, Semen Bogdanov, Teddy Crawford, Terry-Ann Taylor.

Fourth, my advanced readers who gave me lots of insights and suggestions that brought the final pieces of the book together.

Finally, you. Thank you for reading my book. You have a lot of shit to get done, and I'm happy my story is one of them. I hope you were able to laugh and learn through my adventures and misadventures. Thank you!

I've got some shit to get done and so do you. I'm signing off now!

Georgie OUT!

December 2018

Catch me on social at @gsdwithgeorgie or making cool things online at Gsdwithgeorgie.com or email me at georgie@gsdwithgeorgie.com

AUTHOR BIO

My name is Georgie-Ann Getton-Mckoy. I'm the Execution Strategist. That means that I analyze your current resources and circumstances to help you build a realistic and attainable plan to execute on your business idea or project.

In my personal life, I'm a Mom of 2 and a wife. In my professional life, I'm a serial entrepreneur, community builder, speaker, author, and a Diversity in Tech Enthusiast. I hold a B.S. in Business Communications with a specialization in Graphic Communications from Baruch College and a Certificate in Entrepreneurship Essentials from HBX | Harvard Business School. I enjoy learning as well as teaching new and creative ways to find solutions to problems.

I was born in Kingston, Jamaica. At the age of seven, my Mom, two brothers, along with various uncles, aunts, and cousins all immigrated to the US. The majority of my time was spent living in the Bronx, NY, but at the age of 15, my mother sent me to live with my father's side of the family who resided in Baldwin & Freeport, NY. I resisted the entire move, but unknown to me, my life was about to change forever.

The Baldwin Community and the school opened my eyes to what I'd only seen on TV thus far - affluent black people who were in upper-middle-class or merely rich. I saw the "American Dream" that so many had talked about, and it seemed more attainable than ever at this point. I started warming up to this community, and they accepted all my ways that, in the past, were labeled as "nerdy and quirky". I was feeling motivated and welcomed!

Six months later, I turned 16 and became pregnant while in the 11th grade. At this time, I made a decision that would change the rest of my life. With doubts, fear, shame, and disappointment oozing from family and friends around me, I realized it was time to activate my "Getting Sh*t Done" aka GSD abilities.

My life has been a beautiful rollercoaster since. From launching various companies, some failing miserably, to others making over $100k, being on food stamps, suffering from depression, graduating college, attending Harvard, and much more.

Now at the age of 24, I've continued to Get Shit Done and teach others how to do the same regardless of their resources or circumstances.

Made in the USA
Las Vegas, NV
15 November 2021

34455445R10116